ST. P CORINTH; A BIBLE READER'S GUIDE

by

Richard E. Davies

Ina and Elsie Memorial Publication
Morrow, Georgia

St. Paul's Corinth: A Bible Reader's Guide
©2010, Richard E. Davies

Sources of photographs, maps, drawings, and other pictorial material are indicated in the captions. Map, p. 70, courtesy Dr. M. J. T. Lewis. Other identified pictorial materials are believed to be in public domain. Pictorial materials without identification are property of the author.

Contact the author at:
6610 Peacock Blvd., Morrow, GA 30260

To all the "regulars" at the Network of Biblical
Storytellers, especially Ellen
in the office at Christian Theological Seminary.

Corinthian coins:
Pegasus drinking at Peirene Fountain,
        Bellerophon capturing the flying horse,
        and Pegasus fighting the monster.
        (Imhoof-Blumer and Gardner, plate C.)

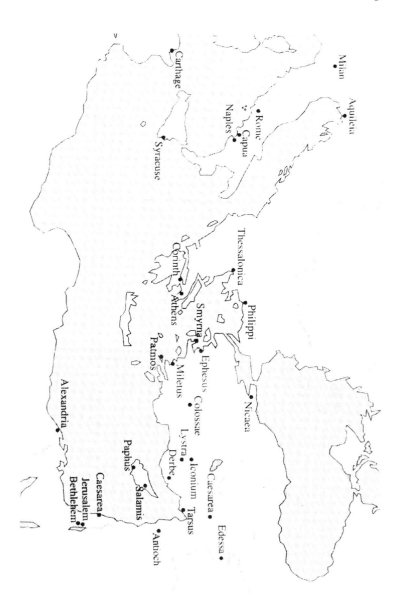

Milan

Aquileia

Carthage

Naples

Rome

Capua

Syracuse

Thessalonica

Corinth

Athens

Smyrna

Philippi

Patmos

Ephesus

Miletus

Colossae

Nicaea

Alexandria

Lystra

Iconium

Paphus

Derbe

Caesarea

Salamis

Caesarea

Jerusalem

Bethlehem

Tarsus

Edessa

Antioch

St. Paul's Corinth:
A Bible Reader's Guide.

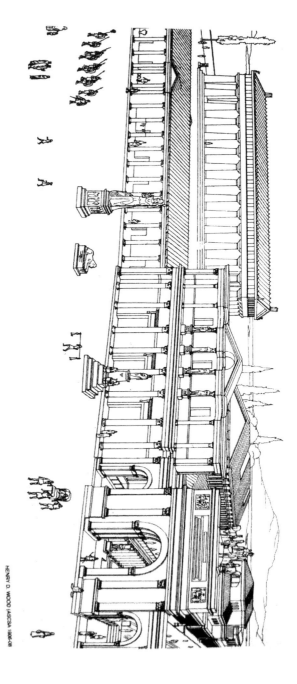

Page 9: Map of the Corinthian Agora (or Forum) and Theatre with notes about changes after St. Paul's visit to the city. Source: Broneer, p. 79.

Page 8: Reconstruction of the north side of the Agora. The road to Lechaeum is through the large arch on the right of the picture. Source: a plaque displayed in ancient Corinth.

HENRY D. WOOD (ASSM 1906-08

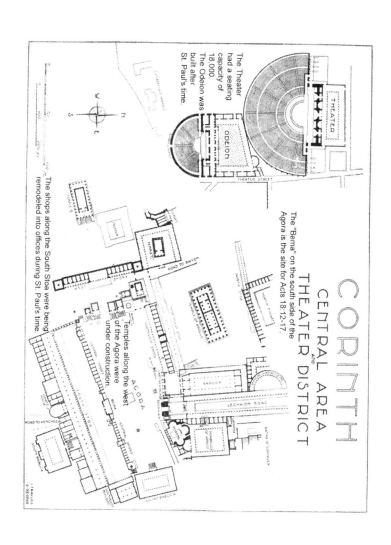

CORINTH
CENTRAL AREA AND THEATER DISTRICT

The "Bema" on the south side of the Agora is the site for Acts 18:12-17.

The Theater had a seating capacity of 18,000. The Odeion was built after St. Paul's time.

Temples along the West of the Agora were under construction.

The shops along the South Stoa were being remodeled into offices during St. Paul's time.

THEATER

ODEION

THEATER STREET

AGORA

BASILICA

LECHAION ROAD

ROAD TO SIKYON

10

PREFACE

First Corinthians is certainly one of the most important books of the New Testament. It is a letter of broad scope. It is a major source for New Testament morality. It presents a developed notion of the link between temporal life and life after death. Our earliest testimony to the Lord's Supper is in this letter. The "love chapter" has had a profound influence on Christian thought and behavior. Second Corinthians, does not carry the impact of First Corinthians, but also has given generations of readers guideposts for life. Among other things, it is the second letter that guides us as we confront financial issues in the temporal church.

Given all of this, it is worth asking about the background of these letters. An entire library of works has been written about the Corinthian letters and about St. Paul. Much less has been written about the Corinthians themselves, and they are the focus of this small book.

What you will find in this book is a set of short intercon-
nected essays that briefly set forth what we know about the
Corinth that St. Paul and his congregation knew, and how the
culture of the city might have influenced both the congregation
and St. Paul's advice to the congregation. As much as possible,
the essays are independent, so that the reader can look at what
seems interesting, rather than being forced to read the entire
book to get one idea. This inevitably means there will be some
redundancy for which the author apologizes. For the most part,
the essays treat aspects of life in ancient Corinth, rather than
treating aspects of Christian life. This means that some topics
of Christian interest appear in more than one essay, and the perspective on the topic will be different in different essays. For
example, the Lord's Supper is mentioned in three essays,
"Common Meals and the Lord's Supper," "Sacramental Drunkenness," and "A Character of Legend."

    The author hopes this essay structure will help the
reader understand the complex culture of Roman Corinth. In
spite of the best efforts of anthropologists to describe culture as
a seamless cloth, it appears to be more of a "crazy quilt," pieced
together from a collection of elements. Any two people in a
large urban "culture" may share a deep interest in one topic, or
a deep concern for one public issue, but we will each have a
totally different set of interests and concerns apart from the one
that joins us. Think of the members of a congregation. Assume
that each has a vital interest in the faith (even though we know
from experience and sociological research that reasons for
church involvement are highly varied), but outside of church,
one attends classical music concerts, another attends rock concerts, one belongs to a classic car club, another rides a bicycle
to work, one reads constantly, another hasn't read a book or a
magazine since finishing high school.

In ancient Corinth there were educated community leaders and laborers with little or no education, there were bankers and tradesmen and athletes, there were housewives and celibate priestesses and ladies of the night, there were makers of bronze and makers of pottery, there were transients and residents, there were residents whose families had come from all over the Roman Empire when the destroyed city had been reestablished fewer than 100 years before St. Paul's visit. St Paul spoke to people from all sectors of society, and people from all sectors responded. The Bible reader should understand these people.

The author is not a New Testament scholar, but a preacher who has scholarly credentials in communication theory, a discipline that emphasizes the importance of understanding the people who receive a message. During approximately 40 years of ministry, the author has found that anyone who would be effective in preaching, teaching, counseling, and church administration must understand the "audience."

This book is not a "commentary." Although it discusses certain passages from the Corinthian letters, it does not discuss every passage, and no passage is discussed exhaustively. Likewise, this book is not an exposition of St. Paul's theology, even though there are essays about aspects of his teaching. The book is an attempt to understand the people in their environment, and how they might understand what St. Paul wrote, given the limitations we face in understanding a different culture from a distance of 2,000 years.

The author has been involved in the "Network of Biblical Storytellers" for more than a quarter of a century, and has come to a deep understanding of the role of our stories in shaping our theological understanding. Thus as we seek to under-

stand the Corinthians, one approach will be to look at the Corinthian stories, and the counter stories that St. Paul no doubt
told.

There are limits on what a book such as this can ac-
complish. Some topics are simply not covered. The ancient belief system included an active belief in demons, but that topic
doesn't seem to be crucial for this book. The role of women in
Corinthian society does not receive much discussion in this
book. Currently there is a great deal of research and scholarly
debate about the role of women in Greek and Roman society,
and at this point there is not enough consensus to provide background for a short structured essay. Likewise, in 21st Century
society there is a great social debate on homosexuality. It is
common knowledge that homosexuality was a recognized part
of Classical Greek society, its place in Roman society is more
problematic, and the great debate about the issue in today's society makes it too complex for the purposes of this book. One
would have to write a long analytical article, not a short essay.[1] The Roman official, Gallio (Acts 18:12-17) is important
to New Testament scholars for dating St. Paul's visit to the city,
but is of little or no importance for St. Paul's message, so this
book has no discussion of him. There is an essay about making
bronze, but no similar essays about the important industries of
pottery or roofing tile. Clearly this book presents a partial view
of the bustling city of commerce and manufacturing!

As the author has sought to understand life and culture
in the "blue collar city of Roman Corinth, he has turned to research in many disciplines, and has attempted to base his writing on scholarly consensus. There is no original research here,
but the author hopes each reader will find information that is
"new" and helps expand the reader's understanding of St.
Paul's writing. The preacher should get a few ideas

from this book that will be useful in developing sermons. The lay person should gain a deeper appreciation for St. Paul, his ministry, and the people who were learning to live in accordance with a religion that was very different from the standard pagan options.

Thanks to the Rev. Gary Vencill who read and critiqued several of the essays, and thanks to Google. Without the "Google Scholar" and "Google Books" tools, this book would not have been possible. Thanks also to libraries at Emory University and Clayton State University. Dina Kastrinakis, our treval agent in Greece, has provided invaluable help. Special thanks to my wife, Elaine, for "putting up with me" during the writing, and for proof-reading the "final" version. Any errors are certainly not her fault!

---

[1] Furnish has written a good analytical article on homosexuality in the world of St. Paul. It is 30 pages long, and concludes, among other things, that "there is no evidence that [St. Paul] ever had to deal with a specific case of homosexual conduct." (p. 78.)

Small temples on the west end of the Agora. Some of
these were under construction when St. Paul visited Corinth.

INTRODUCTION

The Lay of the Land

Why Corinth? Corinth is located on an isthmus that controlled East-West trade between Asia Minor (Ephesus) and Italy (Rome). Similarly it controlled North-South trade between Attica (Athens) and the Peloponnese (Sparta). In addition, the geology of the isthmus supported many springs. In the earliest days there was adequate water for farming, and in later times there was adequate water for a large city. Geography and geology were the reasons for the greatness of Corinth.

In ancient times, it was much safer to transport goods, and sometimes entire ships, across the isthmus than to go around the Greek peninsula, and this transport was so popular that the Corinthians built a road across the isthmus on which goods were transported for almost 700 years. The Emperor Nero and Alexander the Great each tried to dig a canal across the isthmus, but the task was too difficult for ancient engineering. A canal was finally dug in 1893.

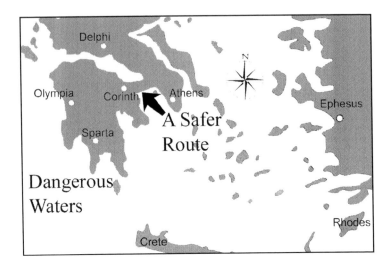

When you visit ancient Corinth, the first thing you notice is a mountain that rises abruptly out of the plain. It is called the Acrocorinth, and formed the Western boundary of the ancient city. It provided a barrier against attack from the West, and a potential refuge in case of attack from another direction. In fact, it was never used as a refuge for the people, but it had potential. It was a fairly short walk from the "downtown" area ("forum" or "agora") to the base of the Acrocorinth, and we can be sure that going to the summit was a common activity. It would have been like going to a city park.

There were several pagan temples on the way up. When St. Paul was there, some of them would have been old, some would have been new, and some were under construction. On top of the mountain was a famous temple where the goddess of love, Aphrodite watched over the city. Much of what we know about Corinth under the Roman Empire comes from an ancient travel guide written by Pausanias, who visited the city about 100 years after St. Paul. Pausanias says, "On the summit of the

Acrocorinthus is a temple of Aphrodite. The images are Aphrodite armed, Helius, and Eros with a bow."[1] Perhaps it seems strange that the "goddess of love" would be armed, but the statement is open to interpretation. Coins show Aphrodite apparently looking at her own image reflected in a polished shield, possibly admiring herself.[2]

The isthmus also had two good natural harbors, one on each side, and the busy harbor towns of Lechaeum and Cenchreae[3] grew up as suburbs. St. Paul mentions a congregation in Cenchreae, where one of the leaders was Phoebe. (Rom 16:1) A third suburb hosted the Isthmian Games which were held every other year and attracted competitors from all over Greece.

Recovering Lost Memories

St. Paul was visiting a "new" city with a complex history, and that complex history is important to us as we try to understand the cultural assumptions of the members of the Corinthian congregation. In many cases, evidence we have about Corinthian culture comes from several centuries before St. Paul. Of course we have to ask whether and how culture changed over

The mountain called the Acrocorinth behind the ruins of the ancient city.

the centuries, but the question is especially important when we seek to understand culture in the "new" city of Corinth.

For reference, let's look at the way historians and archeologists define some time periods in the life of ancient Corinth and the Isthmus:[4]

700 BCE to 480 BCE – The Archaic Period
480 BCE to 323 BCE – The Classical Period
323 BCE to 031 BCE – The Hellenistic Period
031 BCE to 250 CE – The Early Roman Period

The Classical Period was when Greek philosophy and drama thrived. For example, the philosopher Plato lived 430-347, and the tragic dramatist Euripides had his first play produced in 455. We will suggest that both of these people are important for our understanding of St. Paul's Corinth, even though they lived several hundred years earlier. The Cynic philosopher, Diogenes, lived in Corinth in the early 300s, and we will also suggest that he was remembered in St. Paul's time, more than 300 years later. In general, the culture of Classical Greece was still a vital force in Roman Corinth.

Our assumptions are complicated by the destruction of Corinth in 146 BCE. Several ancient authors tell us that Corinth was completely leveled and that the Greek isthmus was a wasteland for 102 years, until Julius Caesar reestablished it as a new Roman colony in 44 BCE. For 2,000 years, schoolchildren have been taught about the cruel destruction of the great city of Corinth by the vengeful Roman general, Lucius Mummius, and poets such as Byron have lamented the great city's passing. In the early 20th Century, historian Willis West wrote, "The destruction of Corinth was a greater crime than that of Carthage,

Syracuse, Capua, or the other capitals that Roman envy laid low. Corinth was a great emporium of Greece, and its ruin was due mainly to the jealousy of the commercial class in Rome."[5] When Julius Caesar reestablished the city, he brought in a new population, many of whom had been slaves, and who were moved as freedmen to Corinth. Some authors assume that they had no loyalty to "old" Corinth.

Did this new Corinthian population share any of the culture of Hellenistic or Classical Corinth? If they were establishing a new city, would the heritage of the site on which they constructed the new city have any meaning for them? For example, they would still use the Peirene fountain, but would the legendary history of the fountain become part of their collective memory? Our initial reaction is to say that the "new" would not remember the "old," but this reaction has to do with our own "future shock"[6] culture. Since about 1950, the pace of cultural change has increased rapidly, and we feel that we can bulldoze a city, bring in new people, build a new city on the site, and history will start anew. This is not completely true, but the point we need to recognize is that our assumptions about cultural change do not hold true for most places and times.

Certainly culture has always changed. A striking example is found in the biblical book of Ruth, where the narrator finds it necessary to explain a custom that had evidently been forgotten: "Now this was the custom in former times in Israel concerning redeeming and exchanging . . ." (Ruth 4:7). Likewise, Forbes tells us that popular religious sentiment changed during the century after St. Paul's visit, so that we have to be careful in explaining what St. Paul said by referring to later authors.[7] Forbes also cautions about using earlier authors to describe culture in St. Paul's Corinth. Yes, the burden of proof is on any author who would explain culture in terms of what we know from prior or subsequent centuries. We need to be careful.

Having set up a caution light, let's return to the question of cultural continuity in ancient Corinth. During the last quarter of the 20th Century, archeologists began to question the ancient testimonies about the total destruction of Corinth. We had been told that the entire population was either murdered or sold into slavery and the city was leveled. It turns out that these ancient testimonies were not true, and we can look back and see that these ancient authors were biased.[8]

For one thing, General Mummius assembled his troops outside the city and then waited for two days before entering. The citizens had time to flee. For another thing, the general didn't have the equipment it would have taken to utterly level the city. Notice that they did not destroy the ancient temple of Apollo that remained visible even after the ancient city had been covered with debris. Not only did they not destroy the temple that was a major symbol of the city, archeologists have found that much of the city remained habitable. (Several hundred years after St. Paul's visit, the site was abandoned because of earthquakes.)

The biggest problem Corinth had between 146 and 44 was that it was no longer a political entity. It could no longer govern itself, and the Empire paid it no official attention.
Even so, we have a growing body of evidence that people continued to live and even prosper on the site. Business was conducted there. Goods were transported across the isthmus. The populace imported fine wine. And most important for our concern about cultural continuity, there continued to be some sort of worship at the shrine of Aphrodite at the summit of the Acrocorinth, at the temple of Demeter and Kore (the focus of

worship was shifting from Demeter to Kore), and at the temple of the god of healing, Asclepius. When the city was reestablished as a Roman colony in 44, the old sacred sites continued to be important, even if the focus of the worship changed somewhat over time.

Julius Caesar's reestablishment was a little less than 100 years before St. Paul's sojourn, and much reconstruction was going on at the time of his visit. Some of the old religious sites were being remodeled, such as the temple of Demeter and Kore, and the seaport temple of Poseidon. New temples to "new" gods were being constructed. It must have been an exciting time to be there, but the "old downtown" would have been recognized by someone visiting from the Hellenistic, or even from the Classical period.

Cultural continuity in Corinth seems to have been surprisingly robust, and it seems likely that this continuity would have included a civic memory of the central myths that go back to Archaic Corinth and earlier. Pausanius, visiting a hundred years after St. Paul, found people for whom these myths were still vital. It is to these myths that we turn now.

The Stories People Told

In any society, there are stories that we all know, and these stories define our society's attitudes toward life. These stories are sometimes "historical" and sometimes "mythological" or "fictional." It makes no difference as far as their power to influence our attitudes. For example, in the brief history of the United States of America people have come to tell the fictional stories of the youthful Abraham Lincoln walking a long distance to return a penny that he had mistakenly overcharged a customer and of the young George Washington impulsively chopping down a special cherry tree to test his new axe, and then confessing the deed to his father. We also tell the historical stories of Washington refusing to become a king and of Lincoln delivering the Gettysburg Address from a manuscript penned on the back of an envelope. These are stories of hard work, humility, truthfulness and in the end, optimism. Indeed, whether or not these values truly characterize the typical U.S. citizen, they are values every citizen of the country idealizes.

What, then, about the citizens of Corinth? The Corinthians had a reputation as fun-loving, and Corinth was considered a "wide-open" town where a seaman or sports fan could find whatever pleasure appealed to him. It's worthwhile to ask if this is the way the Corinthians really were. Were they intrinsically happy? Were they optimistic?

About 100 years after St. Paul, a writer of a travel-guide (yes, they had tourists and travel books in the ancient world) visited the city. One of the things Pausanias, as he was named, said about the city was that in memory of two children whom the citizens had killed (back in mythological time), "a figure of Terror was set up. This figure still exists, being the likeness of a woman frightful to look upon."[9] He goes on to say that the new residents no longer made offerings in atonement for killing these children, but this one statue, "Terror," that ordinary people might see every day as they went to work, might be a potent symbol and give us a clue to the outlook of the people of Corinth.

We will return to the murder of the children shortly, but first it makes sense to look at the mythological beginning of the city.

King Sisyphus is said to have founded the city, and he was known as a clever man and capable ruler. For example, once someone stole his cattle, but he had carved a sign into the hoof of each, so could identify them and get them back. In another myth, the goddess Hera drove a man mad so that he killed his son. The man's wife, in an attempt to save their other son, Melicertes, took him in her arms and jumped into the sea. The boy's body washed up on the Corinthian shore, and King Sisyphus buried him. Subsequently he founded the Isthmian Games in the boy's honor. (So even the games were a memorial to a horrible death.)

The main story of Sisyphus had to do with a girl named Aegina. The lustful king of the gods, Zeus, abducted Aegina, and Sisyphus found out about it. Her father was a river god, and opportunistic Sisyphus bargained to tell the river god where to find Aegina if the god would establish a water supply on the summit of the Acrocorinth. Sisyphus then told the girl's father, thus causing the wrath of Zeus to fall on him. Clever Sisyphus was able to avoid punishment for quite some time. First, Zeus sent Death to take him, but he managed to bind death and no person died while death was in chains. Finally Zeus freed death, and sent him after Sisyphus again. This time, Sisyphus instructed his wife not to make the usual offerings for the dead. Therefore he could not rest in Hades because of the lack of offerings, so he convinced Pluto to let him return to life so as to discipline his "neglectful" wife. Thus he returned and lived to an old age. However, the gods had their revenge when he finally died: as we all know, he was punished by having to eternally push a rock up a hill, but never reaching the top.

The son of Sisyphus, named Glaucus, loved horse racing. Somehow he incurred the wrath of Aphrodite (even though she was a "goddess of love," she often showed a mean streak), and the goddess caused his horses to tear him apart.

The son of Glaucus was Bellerophon, who captured and tamed the flying horse, Pegasus. The story is that he had killed a Corinthian citizen and fled to another country where he became a servant of a prominent man. The man's wife lusted for young Bellerophon, but he did not give in to her. She then complained to her husband (just as Potiphar's wife complained about Joseph). The man sent Bellerophon on a suicide mission to kill what we'll call a "dragon," but the goddess Athena gave him a bridle with which to tame Pegasus so he could come down on the beast from the air. Bellerophon and Pegasus then succeeded at two more "suicide" missions, and Bellerophon was given half a kingdom. So far, so good, but Bellerophon decided that he was like a god, and tried to fly Pegasus to the home of the gods. Zeus, not to be trifled with, sent a gadfly to bite Pegasus, so that the horse threw Bellerophon. He survived the fall, but was blinded and wandered homeless for the rest of his days.

It is said that Bellerophon captured Pegasus as the horse was getting a drink at the Spring of Peirene in Corinth, so Corinthian coins always showed an image of Pegasus.

This brings us to the story of Peirene. The spring was one of the main water sources for the city, and many Corinthians went there daily. World-famous Corinthian bronze was said to be so good because it was tempered in the water of Peirene. A woman named Peirene is said to have had two children by the sea-god Poseidon (the two ports of Corinth are named for these children), but somehow the goddess Athena killed one or both of them. Peirene was inconsolable, and she cried so much that she was transformed into the spring.

Another Corinthian water source is also connected with a tale of tragedy, but we need some background for that story. People who know nothing else of mythology know that Jason was the first long distance sailor. He gathered together a crew of heroes, called Argonauts, and sailed to Colchis at the far end of the Black Sea, where he sought the Golden Fleece. At Colchis, the king's daughter was a witch named Medea, and she fell in love with Jason, so she helped him steal the Golden Fleece and, by a very cruel trick, helped him get away from Colchis. There were many adventures on the long voyage, but Jason and Medea returned to Corinth for ten good years and had two children. Then Jason fell in love with an new girl, Glauce, daughter of King Creon, so he divorced Medea. As a wedding present, witch Medea gave Glauce a beautiful gown which caused the wearer to burn. Glauce tried it on, and jumped into a spring to seek relief. She drowned, and the spring has been known as Glauce ever since.

Next, the children of Jason and Medea were killed. Who did it? Many stories say that Medea killed them, but many Corinthians believed that their people committed the murder, and this brings us to the statue of "Terror" we mentioned above. To atone for the murders, the Corinthians held an annual ceremony until the time the city was destroyed: Seven boys and seven girls were dressed in black and had to live for a year in the sanctuary of Hera. At the end of their time, a black she-goat was killed with the knife used to kill the children of Medea, and the goat was burned as a sacrifice.[10] This was also the place where the statue of "Terror" was erected, a statue that survived the time of destruction and was clearly in place when St. Paul was in the city.

As for Jason, he spent the rest of his life as a vagabond, until one day he returned to the Isthmus and sat down in the shade of his old ship, the Argos. The timbers were rotten, and the prow of the ship collapsed on Jason and killed him.

No matter where you were in Corinth, you could see (and still can see) the Temple of Apollo, and you might be reminded daily of its story. Marsyas was a Satyr or Silenus, one of those half-man, half-goat creatures. He found a magical flute that had been crafted by the goddess Athena. She had decided she didn't like it and had thrown it away. Since it was godly, it made beautiful music, and Marsyas "wowed the crowds" wherever he went. Somehow, he and the god of music, Apollo, got into a music contest. (It's not clear who challenged whom.) It was a tie until Apollo turned his lyre upside down and played. You can do that with a stringed instrument, but you can't do it with pipes, and Marsyas lost that last round. The wager had included the provision that the winner could do whatever he wanted with the loser, so Apollo tied Marsyas to a tree and skinned him alive. The flute (or pipes) ended up in the Temple of Apollo.

Pausanias tells us that a city a few miles north, Sicyon, also claimed the pipes, even though they had since disappeared,[11] but of course the civic pride of Corinth would be unlikely to give way to Sicyon. Thus, the Temple of Apollo became another daily reminder of tragedy and cruelty.

Turning from mythology to history-of-sorts, Herodotus (who sometimes exaggerates) tells tales of Periander, one of the "seven sages of Greece." He is said to have begun his rule over Corinth by systematically murdering all of the leading citizens of the city. He also murdered his wife, but later didn't know where to find something important. Like many husbands, he depended on his wife to keep track of his things, so he called up her ghost to ask her where the lost article was. She refused to tell him, because she was cold in the grave and wanted to get warm.

Periander could take care of that. He called on all of the women and young girls of Corinth to appear at the Temple of Hera, so they came in their best clothes, thinking it must be a celebration. Armed guards surrounded the temple, and the ladies were ordered to strip naked. Periander had a pit dug, threw the clothes in and burned them. His wife's ghost, now warm, told him where to find whatever he had lost.

Did Herodotus tell us the facts? This question doesn't matter, the only thing that matters as far as the Corinthian worldview is concerned is what the people thought was their heritage, what stories they told.

Such are the stories that Corinthians told, and it seems likely that they still told them after the Roman reestablishment, because Pausanias collected many of them and put them in his book. Some he got from literature and maybe he got some from people outside of Corinth, but he probably heard many from Roman Corinthians.

Corinth was one of the wealthiest cities in the ancient world, and it may have been the city of "pleasure," but were the Corinthians happy? Were they optimistic? Did they have a sense that the gods loved or favored them?

---

1 Pausanias, p. 271

2 See the essays "Aphrodite and Her Girls," and "World Class Bronze."

3 The spellings of "Cenchreae" and "Lechaeum" are based on the Jones translation of Pausanias (Loeb Classical Library). "Lechaion" is the spelling used on a sign in ancient Corinth.

4 Kardulias, p. ix.

5 West, p. 394.

6 The phrase was coined by Alvin Toffler for the title of a book about rapid cultural change: Toffler, 1970.

7 Forbes, pp. 2-3.

8 The summary that follows is based on Gebhard and Dickie.

9 Pausanias, p. 263.

10 Furley, p. 137.

11 Pausanias, p. 287.

JEWS –
RESIDENT STRANGERS
WITH A SPECIAL STORY

Among the residents of repopulated Corinth were Jews, probably both slaves and freedmen. There have been many estimates of the population of Corinth in St. Paul's time, and they vary widely, but let's assume the total population (men, women, children and slaves) between 30,000 and 80,000. Let's also assume that Jews comprised 10% of this population, between 3,000 and 8,000. How many synagogues would this many Jewish residents require? Certainly more than one. If archeological work on the city continues, someday a synagogue will be found, and Christians will say, "Now we know where Titus Justus or Gaius lived."[1] Maybe, maybe not.

Whether members of the congregation of Gaius, or some other congregation, the Jews of Corinth were Hellenized: they spoke Greek and they thought in terms of Greek ideas. They made daily trips to the Fountain of Peirene, they passed by the Temple of Apollo and the statue of "Terror," and they traded in coins featuring Pegasus, but in their synagogues they told stories that were quite different from the Corinthian stories.

Instead of Bellophron, they told the story of Joseph. Both were wrongfully accused of adultery, both had to endure punishment, both triumphed and became leaders with great authority, but Bellophron succumbed to pride and ended tragically while Joseph served those over whom he exercised power and was able to save his people from famine.

Both Sisyphus and Marsyas contested against the gods, and both of them lost the contest. Instead of these stories, the Jews told about Jacob wrestling with God and being given a new, good, triumphant name, "Israel." The message is that God is not "out to get you," a message that was utterly strange to the pagans.

Jason made a long journey and found a witch wife whom he eventually wanted to leave. Jacob made a long journey, found wives, spent his life with them and established a people.

The Corinthians told of Periander contacting the ghost of his murdered wife to get the answer to a trivial question, and the Jews told of King Saul contacting the ghost of Samuel to learn how to save himself and (he thought) his nation. In both cases the ghost was uncooperative, but Periander placated the ghost by robbing and disgracing the people over whom he ruled, while Saul simply learned of his impending death in battle. Consider the contrasting lessons of these two ghost stories. Take responsibility for your own life, do good, and leave the departed alone.

Throughout the Roman Empire, pagans who were tired of the Greek/Roman gods were attending synagogues to learn different stories. Such people were especially open to the optimistic stories that St. Paul told.

---

1 See Acts 18:7 and Romans 16:23, as well as the essay in this book, "Individuals of Note."

Statue in the Bema, the administrative center of the Roman Colony of Corinth. (See Acts 18:12. KJV calls it the "judgment seat.")

WHAT KIND OF EDUCATION DID ST. PAUL HAVE?

Scholarly analyses of St. Paul fill a library, and it is certainly beyond the scope of a small book about ancient Corinth to summarize the heated debates that have raged and still rage around the personality of the Apostle, but if we are to understand the Corinthian congregation, we must not only understand the people, but the Apostle. Intellectually speaking, where did he "come from." Was he primarily Hebrew or primarily Greek? Did he write from a Hebrew background or a Greek background?

Of course he spoke to both Jews and Greeks. The congregation was started after he spoke in a synagogue.[1] There were three types of people who worshipped in Greek synagogues: People who were Jews by birth, people who had converted to Judaism (proselytes), and people who were sympathetic to Jewish teaching, but had not yet converted ("God-fearers"). Which of these followed St. Paul into the new congregation? We are told that Crispus, a leader of the synagogue followed him and brought his household into the congregation (Acts 18:8), but we don't know about other synagogue worshippers. Perhaps most of those who came from the synagogue were "God-fearers."[2] Perhaps some of them were proselytes who, even though they had become Jewish, were not fully "converted."[3]

Beyond the synagogue, St. Paul also attracted pagan Greeks to the congregation. Some of these were probably people he contacted in the shops of the Agora (or Forum).[4] These would have been working-class people. Some were upper-class people, possibly such as Erastus.[5] We don't know how he contacted upper-class people, but he did and they responded to his message.

The message had to be presented in such a way that all of these varied people would understand. (1) Educated Greeks would most likely respond to classically phrased rhetoric and logic. Even though St. Paul claimed not to have used classically framed teaching (I Cor. 2:1), we see evidence of it in his letters. (2) Working-class Greeks would have responded to emotional appeals similar to those of the mystery religions. (3) Those raised and educated as Jews would have responded to rabbinic forms of argument.

What kind of background did St. Paul have that enabled him to speak meaningfully to each of these three groups? As a working tradesman, his every-day experience had no doubt taught him how to speak to working-class people. Furthermore, he was subject to mystical experience (II Cor. 12:1-10), so he could speak "from the heart" to working-class people oriented to mystery religions.

At the same time, he was able to speak to philosophically oriented upper-class Greeks and to theologically-oriented

Jews. What in his background enabled him to relate intellectually to such people? This is a much debated question, and we have to admit that we can only guess.[6]

A Jewish scholar, Joseph Klausner, says, "To be sure, Paul the apostle did not formally study 'Greek learning,' in spite of the verses from Aratus, Epimenides, and Menander which he is said to have quoted or which he actually did quote. Like all the Sages of Israel, Paul despised that learning; for it was not religious and devout but pagan and profane . . . I doubt very much if he had any knowledge of the current philosophy of the period, the Stoic and Cynic . . ."[7]

In contrast, another Jewish scholar, Hyam Maccoby, considers St. Paul's quotations from Greek literature to be evidence for Greek learning.[8] Maccoby argues forcefully that St. Paul never studied rabbinic learning, disagreeing explicitly with Klausner. According to Klausner, the epistles carry evidence that St. Paul spoke Hebrew fluently,[9] while Maccoby doubts that he knew Hebrew, even though he had learned Aramaic at home in Tarsus.[10]

In any case, whether St. Paul was educated in the school of Gamaliel, or whether the testimony attributed to him was reported incorrectly, (Acts 22:3) both Klausner and Maccoby demonstrate that he had learned enough about rabbinic styles of debate that he could persuade some of those who were open to rabbinic arguments.

For example, Klausner points to St. Paul's use of the story in Exodus 34:29-35, about Moses veiling himself because his face shown brightly after his meeting with God. In II Cor. 3:7-18, St. Paul uses this story as an analogy of the appearance of the Spirit of God to the followers of Jesus. Klausner would

38   *Preliminary Considerations*

not agree with St. Paul's interpretation, but he concludes that, "This interpretation is typically Midrashic in its form, and is changed from a Jewish to a Christian interpretation only by its deliberately altered content."[11]

Maccoby tells us that rabbinic logic was different from Greek logic especially in the way it used analogy. The rules for use of analogy in rabbinic debate were subtle, but when used properly they were considered sufficient to prove a point. In Greek logic, analogy is never considered sufficient to prove anything. For Greeks, analogy illustrates, it doesn't prove. St. Paul's statement about Moses in II Cor. 3:7-18 appears to be the rabbinic form of argument by analogy. Maccoby says that St. Paul seldom uses this form of argument properly (and Maccoby does not comment on II Cor. 3:7-18), but even if he used the argument improperly, he knew enough of the form to present the argument. In other words, he was not entirely ignorant of rabbinic debate.

Here are another couple of examples of St. Paul speaking to those who were looking for "Jewish" style arguments: Klausner calls attention to I Cor. 9:9-11 (the same argument is in I Tim. 5:17-18), which quotes Deut 25:4 about how to treat a beast of burden, and applies it to preachers of the gospel. He comments, "Here again we have Jewish exegesis of the usual kind."[12] St. Paul's teaching about the resurrection of a "spiritual body" (I Cor. 15:44-46) also betrays his Jewishness, according to Klausner. St. Paul's conclusion is a "non-Jewish and almost an anti-Jewish point of view," because, unlike St. Paul, Jews did not reject the body in favor of the spirit, even though they debated about the relationship between flesh and spirit. The reason St. Paul ultimately rejected the "flesh" is because of his Greek background.[13]

So St. Paul may have been educated in a rabbinical school, or he may have had an incomplete rabbinical education, or he may have simply "picked up" some basic principles of rabbinic argument from informal theological debates and attending synagogue services.

What about his education in Greek logic and rhetoric? The conclusion is the same: maybe or maybe not. In another essay in this book, we make the point that St. Paul was apparently familiar with Greek logic, even though he may not have used it correctly.[14]

Classen makes a sensible observation that can serve us well as we try to understand how St. Paul spoke so convincingly to so many audiences. Classen speaks of rhetoric, but it applies also to logic:

> (a) Anyone who could write Greek as effectively as Saint Paul did must have read a good deal of works written in Greek, thus imbibing applied rhetoric from others, even if he never heard of any rules of rhetorical theory; so even if one could prove that Saint Paul was not familiar with the rhetorical theory of the Greeks, it can hardly be denied that he knew it in its applied form;
>
> (b) Anyone who studied the Old Testament as carefully as Saint Paul undoubtedly did must have noticed the rhetorical qualities displayed there and must have given some thought to the best way of expressing himself.[15]

We cannot be certain how St. Paul was educated (or what "academic degrees" he held), but he was clearly intelligent and gifted, with a gift of being able to speak convincingly to a wide variety of people.

1 Acts refers to *the* synagogue, but there must have been more than one in a city the size of Corinth with its large population of Jews.

2 Titus Justus, who provided space for the congregation, was one of these. (Acts 18:7) Gaius and Titus Justus may have been the same person. See Goodspeed's article in the bibliography.

3 Klausner, pp. 48-49.

4 The Classical Greeks called the city center the "agora," while the Romans called it a "forum." Archeologists are pretty certain that in ancient Corinth the old city's "agora" and the new city's "forum" were located in the same place, and we will sometimes call it one term, and sometimes the other.

5 See the essay, "Individuals of Note."

6 Hock argues that St. Paul was uncomfortable with his low-class tent-making trade, and this indicates his upper-class background. See essay, "Tent Making and Other Low Class Jobs."

7 Klausner, p. 463. In spite of this, Klausner recognizes that St. Paul "was saturated with the ideas of Plato and the Stoa . . . ideas which were hovering, so to speak, in the air, and were widespread even among non-philosophers." p. 488.

8 Maccoby, p. 215. Notes 9 and 10 give details about these Greek quotations in the epistles, and p. 70 is where Maccoby concludes that St. Paul is "naturally at home in the Hellenistic world."

9 Klausner, p. 458.

10 Maccoby, p. 70.

11 Klausner, p. 455.

12 Klausner, p. 457.

13 Klausner, pp. 486-487.

14 See the essay, "Logic of Goddesses."

15 Classen, p. 323.

"Northwest Shops." We can imagine St. Paul working in a place such as this.

HOUSES AS CHURCH BUILDINGS

Ancient Greek society was based around the idea of "family," so that associations, "clubs," and civic organizations were also seen as families. Furthermore, most associations met in homes. There were meeting-spaces in various temples in Corinth, notably in the Temple of Demeter on the Acrocorinth, and the Temple of Ascepilus, but there were not the sort of church buildings, lodges and other group meeting-spaces that we, in the 21st century, have in all of our towns and cities. Instead, the cities had mansions occupied by the wealthy which housed their personal "families" (including the family slaves), and which were also opened for use by artificial "families." Among these artificial "families" that met in houses were some mystery religions, philosophical schools, associations and synagogues.[1] So it was not remarkable that the congregation started by St. Paul met in someone's house.

We really don't know how this congregation was organized. Although we can be certain that the head of the sponsoring household[2] would have been wealthy, and would likely have been seen by the congregation as a "patron" to whom deference was due, we cannot say to what degree he influenced the theology, form of worship, or the administration of the congregation. We do know from "everyday" experience in our 21st Century congregations that the "tone" of a congregation is influenced not only by the clergy, but also by the informal lay leadership. Among congregations established by St. Paul, Philippi seemed to get along pretty well, while Corinth had real problems. To what degree was the difference attributable to the culture of the city, to what degree was it attributable to the make-up of the congregation's membership, and to what degree was it attributable to the personality of the host? We don't know.

Even though we don't know how the congregation was organized, we do know something about the building, and places of worship are interesting in themselves.

In the early 1930s, archeologists found the only identifiable house-church that we have ever found.[3] It was located in Syria, in the city of Dura-Europus, and was used a couple of hundred years after St. Paul's time. However, we assume that it gives us a clue to what house churches may have been like in other places and times.

The Dura-Europus house is large, with many rooms around an open court-yard.[4] It was probably a two-story structure, so that there was space available in the down-stairs that could be dedicated to congregational worship. Thus, we find that a wall had been taken down to provide a nave (more commonly called a "sanctuary"), and a separate area had been provided for a baptistry.[5]

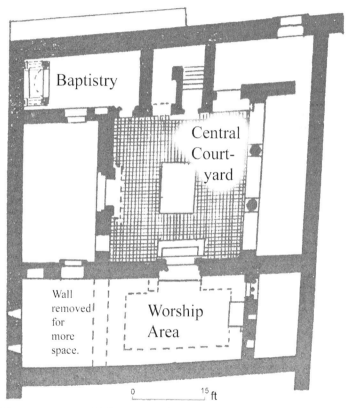

Baptistry

Central Court-yard

Wall removed for more space.

Worship Area

0   15 ft

House Church Floor Plan
Dura-Europus, Syria, about 225 CE

In today's churches we sometimes hear someone speaking wistfully about the "simplicity" of the "early church." They wish our congregations could have such simplicity and, presumably, purity. They will go on to say that we would be better off if we returned to the "house church" concept. No more building maintenance, no more trustees (or whatever their denomination may call those charged with maintaining the congregation's property), no more debates about what to fix, and when to fix it, and what it should look like when it is fixed. This nostalgia for a lost "innocence" can become quite elaborate, but it is misplaced. From its earliest days the church recognized that it needed a fixed place to meet, and within three generations (even before the time of Constantine)[6] it was erecting fairly elaborate buildings.

The United States is a young enough nation that we can "remember" a similar movement. In the early 1800s, frontier preachers met congregations in log cabins, and soon these congregations erected simple "log cabin" style church buildings. (A great argument was whether to have backless benches or pews.) The preacher's children erected simple frame (not "log cabin" style) church buildings. Many of the grandchildren, in the early 1900s, had moved to the city and were gathering for worship in large buildings with choir lofts and balconies. In another generation, they were arguing about the propriety of installing air conditioning in the House of the Lord.

The thing to remember is that in every age the Church has worried about the "worldly" business of meeting space and who should control that space. The members of the Corinthian congregation had to wrestle with such "non-spiritual" matters as much as we do.

1 Maier, p. 15-28.

2 See essay, "Individuals of Note."

3 Stern, p. 914b.

4 The floor plan illustration is based on Davies, 1952, p. 21, and Toynbee, 1969, p. 197. These were based on an illustration in Hopkins. You can find a three-dimensional sketch in Bowes, p. 580.

5 There is a color photograph of a picture above the Dura Europus baptismal font in *The Interpreter's Dictionary of the Bible, Supplementary Volume* (Abingdon, 1976), plate XXXVII. The picture shows the "Good Shepherd" returning a sheep to the flock.

6 The "Edict of Milan" in 313 commanded that church real estate be restored, and the historian Eusebius records a "follow-up" letter from Constantine to his Proconsul in Africa ordering that "those things which these same churches possessed formerly should be restored to them . . . whether gardens or buildings or whatsoever belonged to these same churches." Thus we know that they had buildings and other real estate by the time of Constantine. See Stevenson, pp. 300-303.

A clay household bank from
the time of St. Paul.

PUBLIC AND PRIVATE MONEY

In the ancient world there were no credit cards, but there was credit. There were no checks, but there were acknowledgements of debt. There was no paper money, but there was cash. In other words, finance was a part of daily life, and there were institutions to regulate finance. In particular, there were banks.

Corinth, with its strategic location, its production of desirable bronze and pottery, and its hosting of visitors to the Isthmian Games, required sophisticated financial services. Corinthians had issued coins for several hundred years (always with the image of Pegasus on one side) before the destruction of the city, when the mint was, of course, put out of operation. After Julius Caesar reestablished the city, it became a site for an official mint under the jurisdiction of the Roman Empire. (The mint was shut down briefly under Vespasian in 68/69, almost two decades after St. Paul's sojourn.)[1]

Trade required business loans and insurance, and systems for both of these developed. Insurance was a little different from what we know by that name. There were no insurance companies to "pool" risks. Instead, the need for insurance was taken care of through what has been called "bottomry loans." A merchant who was shipping goods to another port faced a serious risk of losing everything as a result of piracy or severe weather, so they would get a loan for the full value of their merchandise (essentially purchasing the merchandise on credit) with the guarantee that if the cargo was lost, the loan would not have to be repaid. The interest on such a loan was very high, but both parties to the bargain saw these loans as good investments. The concept was invented about the same time that coins were first minted, about 500 BCE, and the system of bottomry loans continued well into the time of the Roman Empire.[2]

Banks were the institutions that made all of this possible. MIT Economist Peter Temin has commented, "Ancient historians and modern economists fortunately employ the same definition of a bank, which makes it relatively straightforward to discuss to what extent loans and banks were present in the early Roman Empire."[3] Banks fulfilled three primary necessities in cities like Corinth: (a) money changing, (b) money lending, and (c) receipt of deposits for safe-keeping or investment.[4] (Interest on loans was normally at the rate of 1% per month, or 12% per year.) In addition, it was fairly common for banks to issue orders to bankers in other locations to pay a certain amount, thus freeing merchants from having to carry large sums in cash (*i.e.*, coins).

This never developed into a system of checking accounts and there were no clearing houses to facilitate the transfer of funds, partly because money was considered to be valuable metal rather than a symbol for credit. It is a bit surprising that nothing like a banking association to facilitate transfer of funds developed, because associations were common in Greek society for all sorts of purposes: business, politics, religion, benevolence and social relationships.

With this background, think about St. Paul's collection for the poor (Gal. 2:10, II Cor. 9) Temin made a study of the price of wheat in the Roman Empire, and even though he didn't emphasize it, his data show that wheat in Palestine was much more expensive than it should have been.[5] Why was the Jerusalem congregation in financial distress? Some have pointed to their experiment with "communism" as the reason (Acts 4:32-5:11), but Temin's study of secular economics suggests that the money simply didn't go far enough.

Although the records of St. Paul's agreement with the Jerusalem congregation are confusing (Acts 15:1-35 and Galatians 2:1-10) it seems clear that he had a concern for the well being of those in Jerusalem. Thus, he collected money to be sent back to Jerusalem, and he felt that Corinth was so wealthy that the Corinthian congregation should provide a substantial portion of the contribution (II Cor 9).

An interesting question is how it was handled. Coins are cumbersome, even though they were necessary in the economic system that existed until our time. Archeologists from time to time find jars full of coins, either a business' capital or someone's life savings.[6]

To understand how bulky the Corinthian contribution might have been, consider that the Aeginetic talent weighed almost 80 lbs. avoirdupois.[7] How likely was it that the Corinthian congregation collected as much as an Aeginetic

Money in the Early
Roman Empire

1 drachm = 6 obols.
An ordinary day's wage
was between
3 obols and 2 drachma.

1 denarius approx. equal to
1 drachm

1 mina = 100 drachma

1 Greek talent =
60 minas,
which is a weight
of 80 lbs. (The talent in
the New Testament Gospels is a little heavier.)

1 Greek silver talent =
about 20 years' wages.

talent? This was equal to 8,280 Attic drachmas, which under the Roman system was also 8,280 dinari (the familiar Gospel money).[8] Generally workers (even skilled workers) were paid between ½ and 2-1/2 drachmas per day, so an Aeginetic talent might represent 25 or 30 years worth of wages for one worker. However, it was not unknown for "special" people to be paid much more than that. One actor is known to have been paid one talent for each appearance.[9] (In the 21st Century, popular actors and athletes still make more for an appearance than the "normal" person will earn in a lifetime.)

Clearly St. Paul was speaking to working class people about the collection when he gave his instructions to set aside each week anything that they had earned in excess of their personal budget (I Cor 16:1-4). If these were the only contributions, they wouldn't begin amount to a talent, but it still seems reasonable that St. Paul hoped for a talent from Corinth.

Suppose the Corinthian congregation had 50 members and they were all "ordinary" workers. In that case, if each pledged 2-years' wages, the collection would total a talent, but that would be too much to ask of them. We know, however, that some of them were from the upper class. There was a great disparity in Greek society between the upper class and the working class. There was almost no middle class. (An architect earned essentially the same wage as a porter.) We know the names of several members of the congregation.[10] Most of those named were probably wealthy (even though people like Prisca and Aquilla were not). Suppose the congregation had five wealthy members. If each of them could contribute 1,500 drachamas, and for wealthy people this would not be unreasonable, the collection would come close to being a talent. The five wealthy would contribute 7,500, and the remainder of the congregation could contribute 780.

The collection from Corinth, in addition to whatever was contributed by the other congregations in Greece and Asia Minor, would be very valuable and tempting to bandits, besides being bulky and extremely heavy. It is quite possible, and maybe even likely, that St. Paul's companions actually transported jars of coins from Greece to Jerusalem. However one wonders if somehow the banking services available in Corinth might have been used to make the transfer of money easier.

---

1 Salmon, p. 171f; Walbank, p. 338.

2 Salmon, pp. 148-149; Edwards, p. 434.

3 Temin, p. 144, fn. 10.

4 Edwards, p. 433.

5 Temin, p. 139, fig. 1. Notice Jerusalem's status as an "outlier," even though Temin doesn't specifically comment on it.

6 For example, see Morgan, p. 541.

7 Ridgeway, p. 444.

8 Not all authorities agree that the drachma and denarius were equal, so we will limit our discussion to the drachma. For more details about money, see Ferguson, p. 85.

9 Edwards, p. 436.

10 See essay, "Individuals of Note."

Tent Making and Other Low Class Jobs

When we visit the ruins of ancient Corinth, we can see several business areas where, it seems, shopkeepers did their trade. It is intriguing to look at these business areas and speculate of whether St. Paul might have made and sold tents out of one of these shops. For example, the "north market" is an area about the size of a football field, with space for more than 50 shops. Imagine St. Paul going to work there each day.

What did he do? Could it have been more profitable in a city such as Corinth to make and repair sails than tents? The skills for the trade would have been the same. (As a matter of fact, no one knows exactly what skills he used. He may have worked with goat-hair cloth or leather.) We can also imagine him taking time away from the trade to wander around the market and talk about faith with other proprietors and with shoppers.

There is nothing wrong with such an exercise of imagination, but some scholars suggest that "tent making" raises a more serious question. How did St. Paul, the tent maker-fit into the cultural expectations of Corinthian society?

For one thing, St. Paul was working at low-status labor. Back home in Tarsus, cloth workers were ordinarily denied citizenship.[1] St. Paul must have been a really special case! For another thing, "important" people did not respect anyone who had to work for a living, no matter what work the person did. E. A. Judge has looked at St. Paul's use of Greek terms, and suggests that he was flouting Corinthian conventions in several ways. One of these breeches of convention lay in his pursuing his own trade. "For reasons which modern Western minds have often found difficult to grasp, they objected to him because he would not accept their support, but insisted on paying his own way by physical labour."[2]

Professor Judge explains that social prestige in the Roman world came, not from making money, but by giving it away. There were several levels of dependence that a recipient might have, and the highest level was called "friendship." The "friend" who received the financial support had the duty to support the donor when it came to any sort of controversy. Judge cites as an example, John 19:12, where Pilate is warned, "If you let this man go, you are not Caesar's friend." Furthermore, says Judge, "if you refused an offer of friendship by not taking someone's money you openly declared yourself his enemy." This is why there seemed to be so much controversy over St. Paul's refusal to accept financial support from the Corinthians.

Some scholars argue that this system of patronage and "friendship" was not the cultural norm outside of Rome and some colonies, so Judge proceeds to develop a detailed argument that the Roman custom was widespread and did apply in Corinth.[3] Other scholars say that it is not surprising that St. Paul worked at a trade, because this was expected of rabbis, but we don't have evidence of rabbis normally working at trades until 100 years after St. Paul.[4]

Another scholar, Gerd Theissen, looks at St. Paul's labor from the point of view of other evangelists who claimed that Jesus had commanded them not to work (Matt. 6:25ff, Matt. 10:40-42, Luke 10:17ff, and related Gospel teachings). Since the other evangelists used their need for support as evidence of their call to preach the Gospel, there were some in the Corinthian congregation who questioned the legitimacy of the preaching of someone like St. Paul who worked for a living.[5]

The question of whether or not labor is respectable is an interesting approach to understanding I Cor. 9, with its somewhat abstract argument that St. Paul had the "right" to receive support from the Corinthians, but he is proud of the fact that "in my proclamation I may make the gospel free of charge, so as not to make full use of my rights in the gospel." (I Cor. 9:18, where the "rights in the gospel" refers to the right of receiving financial support in exchange for preaching the Gospel.)

St. Paul goes on to make a startling statement in the next verse, I Cor. 9:19: "I have made myself a slave to all, so that I might win more of them." What is this "slavery" he is talking about? Is it simply a theological statement, about what it means for anyone to serve Christ, or is it more pointed, expressing some sort of dismay about the need to work? Ronald Hock relates this verse to II Cor. 11:7, "Did I commit a sin by humbling myself . . .?" Hock argues that both St. Paul's "slave" reference and the reference to "humbling" (or demeaning) indicate discomfort with having to work with his hands.[6] This is also reflected in the list of the sufferings endured by the apostles in I Cor. 4:9-13, which includes the phrase, "and we grow weary from the work of our hands." Hock goes on to show that manual labor was considered to be unworthy of an upper class person, and argues that St. Paul's discomfort with having to work is an indication that he truly came from the educated upper class.

Does all of this suggest that St. Paul should not have worked at his trade? No. Working at the trade did at least two good things: it kept him free from being forced to swear allegiance to one or another faction in the divided Corinthian congregation, and it allowed him to have daily contact with working-class people who needed to hear the Gospel.

As far as maintaining freedom is concerned, Hock points out that St. Paul's position had support from some of the eminent writers of the day. Plutarch, Lucian and Epictetus were among those who advised upper class students who were short of money to work, rather than borrow.[7] Of course, few people accepted their advice. Not only was it easier to borrow, it was also more socially acceptable. Hock says, "And so our picture of Paul, of one from the socially privileged classes who when faced with finding support turned to a trade, is historically credible. His behavior was not typical, but it was advocated by moralists and chosen by at least several individuals."[8]

In our time, we sometimes have the opposite problem. Students (especially high school students), who don't need to work, spend valuable study time working at low-paying jobs in order to have luxuries that will elevate their social status among fellow students. When they do that, they increase the likelihood that they will drop out of school, making themselves unemployable in today's economy, or they will graduate with minimal skills and have a difficult time pursuing further education.

Sometimes the story we need to tell is the story of St. Paul making tents in order to preach the gospel, but sometimes the story we need to tell is of the diligent student who studies hard in order to understand the world and, in the service of the gospel, how to make the world a better place.

---

1 Theissen, p. 36, with ref. to Dio Chrysostom.

2 Judge, p. 15.

3 Judge, pp. 16-20.

4 Hock, p. 557.

5 Theissen, pp. 27-53.

6 Hock.

7 Hock, p. 563.

8 Hock, pp. 563-4.

Bronze pots and pans found at Pompeii. (Source: J. Hall, *Buried Cities*, Macmillan, 1923.)

WORLD CLASS BRONZE

Corinth was famous for many things: transportation and trade, banking, the Isthmian Games, Aphrodite's "girls," and also manufacturing high quality pottery and bronze.

Ancient authors from all over, as early as five hundred years before St. Paul, wrote about the bronze made in Corinth. Scholars differ as to what this was, some saying that it was simply bronze manufactured in the city of Corinth, and some saying that the Corinthians had developed a particular composition and method of production of bronze. It seems likely that in the early years they just made good quality bronze, and in later years "Corinthian bronze" was invented as a special product, and still later the formula and method spread so that "Corinthian bronze" was produced in many places. The special alloy known as "Corinthian bronze" may not have been developed until a few decades before Christ. Corinth had a long-standing heritage of producing good quality bronze and a more recent reputation for producing a really special kind of bronze that went back for two or three generations.[1]

In particular, the great gate leading to the sanctuary of the Jerusalem Temple, built by Herod, was made of Corinthian bronze, and Josephus tells us that this gate "far exceeded in value those doors plated with silver and set with gold. This gate was no doubt the "Beautiful Gate" mentioned in Acts 3:2, and was also the Gate of Nicanor mentioned in the Mishnah, which records that the other Temple gates were overlaid with gold, but the bronze of this gate shown like gold without a gold overlay. The gate was the largest thing we know of that was made of Corinthian bronze. Was this Temple gate manufactured in Corinth? Probably not. Most likely it was manufactured in the Egyptian city of Alexandria using techniques developed in Corinth. But for our understanding of Corinth, the important fact is that this particular method of manufacturing bronze was Corinthian. It was part of the city's heritage.

Bronze was also a continuing source of Corinthian wealth. Even though the manufacturing process had been exported to other cities, in St. Paul's time a significant foundry complex where statues were manufactured was located near the gymnasium area.[2] We even have evidence of bronze work in Corinth in the 12th Century, CE, although the special formula seems not to have been used after the second Century.

This bronze really was special. In addition to copper and tin, it apparently contained gold and silver. The ancient writer, Pliny, in his Natural History, says that Corinthian bronze came in three varities: white, nearly like silver; yellow, nearly like gold; a combination of silver and gold; and a fourth variety, "produced by luck," which was valued for portrait statues. It was still being manufactured in the years between Corinth's

destruction and the city's reestablishment, and the Romans valued it highly. Pliny says, "There has been a wonderful mania
among many people for possessing this metal . . . [and Mark
Antony "proscribed" a man] for no other reason than because
he had refused to give up to Antony some pieces of Corinthian
ware."

Unlike the large Jerusalem Temple gate, most of the bronze
was used for statues and small items like plates and cups. In I
Cor. 13:12, St. Paul said, "Now we see in a mirror dimly . . ."
The only mirrors in existence were made of some sort of metal,
preferably bronze. Bronze mirrors had been invented more than
a thousand years before St. Paul,[3] and it would be more than a
thousand years before glass mirrors would be invented.[4] The
bronze mirrors were expensive and precious, but even the best
"Corinthian bronze" mirrors would not show a really good image. St. Paul felt that he was looking at God as if in a bronze
mirror, and longed for a "face to face" view (I Cor. 13:12, II
Cor. 3:18).

There is another thought that might have entered the mind
of a Corinthian when mention was made of "seeing in a mirror
dimly." The statue of Aphrodite on top of the Acrocorinth is
long gone, so we don't know with complete certainty what it
looked like, but we do have ancient coins that seem to depict
that great statue. Pausanias said that the statue was an image of
an "armed" Aphrodite, and we might think this means she was
wearing a suit of armor, but that's not what the coin
shows.[5] On the coin, Aphrodite is nude to the waist, and is
looking at her reflection in a military shield while her son, Eros,
hands her (what looks like) a ribbon, maybe for her hair. Poor
Aphrodite! Trying to get beautiful, but even that great goddess
can only "see in a mirror dimly!" What a contrast with the God
of Abraham!

The Corinthian heritage of bronze production may have been behind St. Paul's reference to "sounding brass" in I Corinthians 13. He said, "If I have not love, I am as sounding brass or a tinkling cymbal . . ." We can imagine what he means by "tinkling cymbal," (even though we may be wrong), but what is "sounding brass?" There are several possibilities.

Maybe the reference is to an ordinary gong. The Arndt/ Gingrich/Bauer Greek-English Lexicon's entry for *chalkos*, definition 2, says, "anything that is made of [copper, brass, bronze] . . . a noisy (brass) gong: I Cor. 13:1." Bronze was thought to have the power to purify, so bronze gongs were used in many kinds of pagan purification rituals.[6]

Maybe St. Paul is making fun of the goddess Demeter, who along with her daughter Kore was very important for the citizens of Corinth. A poet named Pindar referred to her in passing as: "Demeter queen of the ringing brass."[7] This phrase, "queen of the ringing brass," is a single Greek word that is derived from *chalkos*, and translator J. B. Bury says that the word refers to special bronze instruments which were called *echeia*,[8] and "were sounded in the worship of Demeter." These were not the cymbals of Cybele (or Isis), and St. Paul uses a different word, *kumbalon*, for "cymbal." It would make sense that St. Paul might have countered both Demeter and Isis in the same sentence. The European Isis is normally depicted with a noisemaker called a "sistrum" in her raised right hand, and this may also have been called a "cymbal." It certainly looks like something that would have "tinkled."

If the "sounding brass" (or bronze) was a gong or something like it, it certainly would have been manufactured in Corinth, and the reference would have had an impact with the congregation members. But there is at least one more possibility.

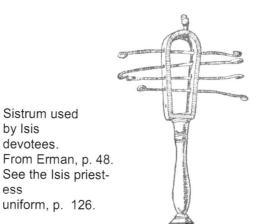

Sistrum used
by Isis
devotees.
From Erman, p. 48.
See the Isis priest-
ess
uniform, p. 126.

Theatres were very important in ancient Greece, and we should remember that they didn't have electronic amplification. Some of the theatres had excellent acoustics, but not all of them. An ancient Roman architect named Vitruvius has left us writings about architectural problems, including instructions for constructing a theatre. He suggests that sound quality will be improved if the stage is lined with a series of tuned bronze vessels, each resonating with a particular note on the scale.[9] Vetruvius goes on to say that even though these bronze vessels were recommended for a really good theatre, they were not used everywhere, probably because large tuned bronze jugs were very expensive. He said, "We cannot point to any in Rome itself, but only those in the districts of Italy and in a good many Greek states." Then he made specific reference to the destruction of Corinth: "We have also the evidence of Roman general Lucius Mummius, who, after destroying the theatre in Corinth, brought its bronze vessels to Rome, and made a dedicatory offering at the temple of Luna with the money obtained from the sale of them."[10] Certainly the theatre of Corinth, home of world famous bronze works, would have the resonating vessels, and when Corinth was rebuilt and the theatre was restored, new vessels would have been installed.

So we have a question: was St. Paul's phrase "sounding brass" a reference to gongs, some sort of musical instrument, or to a sophisticated feature of theatre architecture? We don't know the answer to this question, but we know two things:

First, whatever the reference, the Corinthian congregation would have heard it in relation to their civic pride in world-class bronze production.

Second, whatever the reference, it is clear that "sounding brass" is not able to speak sensibly by itself. Likewise, we need assistance to speak sensibly: the assistance of transcendental "love."

Let's develop this second point: The "gong" or musical instrument associated with Demeter makes no sense without Demeter. The noisemaking cymbal (or sistrum) carried by Isis and her devotees makes no sense without Isis. However, neither of these pagan goddesses make sense anyway, so their "musical" instruments can't make sense.

The resonating vessels in the theatre do no good unless an actor is on the stage providing words to which the vessels can resonate. The actor may make more sense than an idol goddess, but the actor's sense is also limited.

Then put us in place of one of these bronze "things." We can make noise, but not make sense unless God is speaking words of love through us. Unless God is present. Unless we resonate to the loving voice of God.

1 The information about bronze production comes from Jacobson and Weitzman.

2 Mattusch, p. 389.

3 Egyptian bronze mirrors dated as early as the sixteenth century, BCE, are pictured in *The Interpreter's Dictionary of the Bible*, vol. 3 (K-Q), color Plate XVIII.

4 Glass mirrors with metal backing were first manufactured in Venice in the 1700s. "Mirror," The New Encyclopaedia Britannica, Volume 8, (Micropaedia, Ready Reference) 2007.

5 See the coin as part of the essay, "Aphrodite and Her Girls."

6 Harrison, p. 592.

7 Bury, p. 124.

8 See the Arndt/Gingrich/Bauer *Greek-English Lexicon* entry for ἠχέω.

9 These jugs would not amplify sound, but might add clarity to the words being spoken on stage. See Haddad and Akasheh.

10 Vitruvius, Bk. V, ch. 5, par. 8, p. 145.

Corinth canal seen from a train window. Notice how deep it is. Ancient technology could not have completed this project.

MOVING THE MERCHANDISE USING A RAILROAD AND SLAVES

Several thousand years ago the earliest Corinthians probably settled in the area because of rich farmland and ample water supplies. As civilization developed, Corinthians recognized that their location on the isthmus was also a rich resource, as sea trade developed between Asia Minor on the east and the Italian peninsula on the west. Corinth was blessed with good natural ports on both coasts. The small wooden ships of the day could sail along the southern coast of Greece, but it was a somewhat dangerous trip that many ship captains would prefer to avoid. About six-hundred years before Christ the Corinthians built a paved road across the isthmus with grooves in the paving stone that were probably intended to keep the wheels of special carts from going off the road. This arrangement has been called a "railroad," even though it ran on grooves, not rails.[1] This road was called the *Diolkos*, a word which means "haul over" or "transport." It was not unique. There were one or two other such roads in the ancient world,[2] but it was

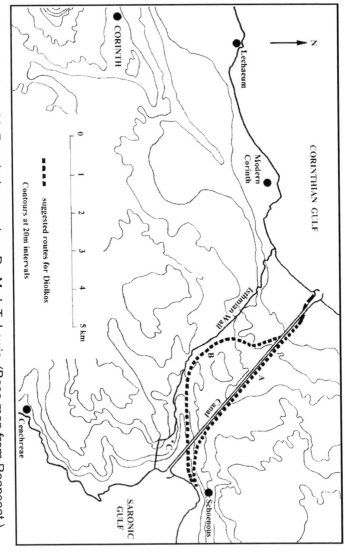

From Lewis, p. 11. Permission courtesy Dr. M. J. T. Lewis. (Base map from Reapseat.)

the best used and most enduring of any of them. Today about
1100 meters of the ancient road have been excavated for us to
see.

The *Diolkos* didn't run between the major natural harbors
of Lechaeum and Cenchreae, but across the isthmus at its nar-
rowest point, connecting two ports specially constructed for the
purpose, fifteen or more miles from the center of town. For
what was the *Diolkos* actually used? The most spectacular use
was to transport warships across the isthmus, but that didn't
happen very often. The reason it was built was to facilitate
commercial trade and provide toll revenue for Corinth. It was
normally used to transport cargo, not ships. The *Diolkos* was
built about the same time as the beginning of monumental construction all over the Greek world, so initially it was apparently
used for heavy cargo, such as marble and timber for constructing temples and government offices. Later it may have been
used to haul smaller cargo ships across the isthmus.[3] An interesting testimony on the question of how much the *Diolkos* was
used comes from the comic dramatist, Aristophanes, who in his
bawdy play, *Thesmophoriazusae*,[4] makes an off-color joke out
of a reference to the frequency of things being transported
across the isthmus.[5] Aristophanes was writing 200 years after
the *Diolkos* was constructed, and clearly he anticipated that
throughout Greece, his audiences would know how goods were
transported over that "railroad."

There is some evidence that the *Diolkos* continued to be
used during the century after the city was destroyed, so we easily assume that full trade was resumed after Julius Caesar reestablished the city, and it was part of the commercial structure of
the city when St. Paul was there. To the best of our

knowledge, it was in regular use until 15-or so years after St. Paul's visit. In the year 67 CE, the Emperor Nero began digging a canal that destroyed part of the *Diolkos*. The canal was beyond the technical capabilities of the day, and was not done until 1893.

It is also a safe guess that the human power necessary to load and unload cargo and drive the ox-carts along the road was the power of slaves, and it is not much of a stretch to imagine that some of these slaves might have joined the congregation in Cenchreae (which was fairly close), if not in Corinth (which was a much longer walk).

Were slaves really that common? Westermann made a thorough review of the evidence, and like so many things in antiquity, the answer is not clear.[6] In the time of the Roman Empire, there was a much more limited supply of slaves than there had been earlier, because prisoners of war were no longer available. The two main sources of Roman slaves were from people "rescuing" unwanted infants who had been exposed to die (the common form of "birth control" in those days) in order to raise them as slaves, and from births within slave families.[7]

As Westermann examined the evidence from various locations (not including Corinth) in the early days of the Roman Empire, it appears that a really wealthy person might have ten or twenty slaves, while most slaveholders might have one or two. In Pergamum in Asia Minor, about 100 years after St. Paul, there was a ratio of one slave per two free adults.[8] It seems that such a ratio might have been a minimum in Corinth.

Slaves did all sorts of work from highly skilled trades to housekeeping and backbreaking labor. For example, in St. Paul's time period the pottery factory at Arretium in Italy was staffed with skilled slaves.[9] Pottery in Corinth might also have been manufactured by slaves. Likewise bronze might have been made by slaves, and Cadbury tells us that some offices of public responsibility were held by educated slaves.[10] Hollenweger includes in his fictional story of Corinth[11] a slave who was employed in the banking business.

Certainly there were a large number of slaves, even if they were a minority, and certainly a good number of strong male slaves were employed moving cargo on the *Diolkos*. Almost as certainly they found fellowship in one or another of the congregations St. Paul established, and that's why he wrote about slavery in I Cor. 7:21-24. However, St. Paul's instruction to remain in whatever state you find yourself raises a problem for us today. There are several things that could be said about this instruction:

> (1) This is the same sort of advice Diogenes the Cynic would have given. We have spoken of Diogenes elsewhere[12] and how the congregation might have been aware of the teachings of Diogenes, but in this case, it seems doubtful that St. Paul had Diogenes in mind in any sense.
>
> (2) The most common 20th Century answer has been to say that St. Paul was expecting the end of the world to come very soon, and that is why he advised everyone that they shouldn't get into new relationships or seek to change their role in this life. There is much that could be said both for and against this approach to understanding St. Paul, but this view doesn't help us in any case. It only makes the passage irrelevant to life as we know it, because we are not going to condone slavery.

(3) More helpful is to look at the situation in Corinth. Under Roman law, most of the slaves could not be set free. Emperor Augustus had put in place a law severely limiting the number of slaves any one person could free. Even in their last will and testament slaveholders were not permitted to free all of their slaves.[13] Furthermore, the Roman authorities were very concerned about the possibility of slave revolts, because the empire had experienced several major ones. St. Paul understood and said several times that in God's eyes, slaves were equal to anyone else (I Cor 12:13, Gal 3:28, Col 3:11, Eph 6:5-9, Philemon), but if he had called for the emancipation of all slaves, the Romans would have seen him as an agitator and he would have been arrested, prosecuted, and executed on the charge, having done no good for the slaves or for the Gospel. Sometimes St. Paul avoided saying things he might have said simply because it would have done more harm than good to say them.[14]

---

[1] Lewis.

[2] Fraser.

[3] See Cook, who argues that the *Diolkos* wasn't used very much, and MacDonald, who responds to Cook saying that the *Diolkos* was used regularly transporting heavy cargo and occasionally transporting ships.

4 The plot has to do with a women's retreat in a temple that is

"crashed" by a man who wants to see what the women are talking about. He is discovered and humiliated. There is no standard English translation for this awkward Greek name. Benjamin Bickley Rogers (1904) called it "Euripides and the Women of Athens." (Rogers edited out the bawdy reference to the Isthmus.) David Barrett (1964) called it "Ladies' Day." Alan Sommerstein (1994) kept the Greek name. The reader should remember that audience for such bawdy plays was exclusively male (except for "ladies of the night").

5 In standard notation, the reference is found in lines 645-650 of the Greek text of the play.

6 Westermann.

7 Westermann, pp. 84ff.

8 Westermann, p. 87.

9 Westermann, p. 92.

10 Cadbury, pp. 51-52.

11 Hollenweger.

12 See essay, "A Character of Legend."

13 Westermann, p. 89.

14 See Kugelman, p. 264.

Athletes on pottery displayed in the National
Archeological Museum in Athens.

CROWN OF VICTORY

Athletic contests were an important part of Greek culture for about 1,600 years from the time of Homer to the time of Emperor Theodosius, who, in the name of Christianity, ordered all pagan worship places to be destroyed. Since the ancient games were in honor of the ancient gods, the destruction of religious sites was equivalent to the destruction of the contests.

There were no team sports in these games. Events included foot-races (including relays, such as the "torch race"), long jump, throwing the discus and javelin, boxing, wrestling, pentathlon, and horse and chariot races. In addition, there were music and poetry contests. This list suggests that the Greek sports were gentle, but that is not the case. When rewards were given, the greatest rewards went to boxing and wrestling, not to track and field. There were no rounds or rest periods in the fighting sports. The action was bloody, went on until one contestant could no longer compete, and it was not unusual for contestants to die during the event.[1]

In the classic era, 500 or 600 years before St. Paul, there were as many as 50 competitions held on a regular basis throughout Greece. By the time of St. Paul, there were still many minor competitions, but there were four important competitions: the Olympic Games, the Pythian Games, the Nemean Games, and the Isthmian Games, and in each of these contests, the prize was a crown of leaves. This is not to suggest that they only got leaves. Cities placed a high value on citizens who could claim a prize at one of the "crown" games, and the athletes were highly rewarded when they returned home. We have a document from Roman Egypt, about 200 years after St. Paul, indicating that the city treasury paid more than 7 talents to successful athletes during one year.[2] Furthermore, at the same time, the Roman emperor, Gallienus, suggested that the descendants of illustrious athletes should have privileges, such as exemption from military duty.[3]

The philosopher, Plato, competed as a wrestler in the Olympics, and continued to be a spectator in later years. At the height of his fame, he shared a tent with strangers because of the shortage of lodging at the Olympic site. His tentmates didn't find out who he was until later.[4]

The adulation of successful athletes was so great that their sweat was marketable. At the end of an event, the athletes would clean themselves by scraping their bodies, getting rid of the sweat and dust that was mixed with the oil they had applied to their bodies before the event. There was even a law regulating the sale of this sweaty substance (called *gloios*), which was thought to have therapeutic and magical properties.[5]

Two of the minor games were established in Palestine by Herod the Great. One location, of course, was the new city of Caesarea Maritima that he constructed, and there he gave cash prizes to first, second, and third-place contenders (the custom was to give an award only to the winner). The games at Caesarea were held every four years for at least a century-and-a-half. More surprisingly, Herod also established a quadrennial contest at Jerusalem. Josephus comments that these games, along with a theatre, and other Jerusalem innovations were "alien to the character of the Jews." Even so, Josephus says, "The celebration of the Games was outstanding . . . Athletes came from all over the world in hope of prizes and the glory of victory." Josephus adds that the Jerusalem stadium also was the site for wild beast shows.[6]

One indication of the importance and prestige of these contests is that slaves were excluded from them.[7] Generally it was the wealthy who had time to train for athletic competiton, but laborers also sometimes competed.[8] Only slaves were excluded. Competitors were expected to be worthy citizens who upheld the highest standards of law and conduct. If a competitor cheated or registered and then backed out of the contest, the penalty was a flogging. This was a punishment normally reserved for slaves, and the flogging of an athlete had the effect of symbolically reducing him to the status of a slave.[9]

The Olympic Games were held every four years, and the Isthmian Games every two years, alternating in competition with the Olympics and the Pythian Games. In particular, the Isthmian Games were held in 47, 49, 51, and 53 CE, so St. Paul was probably in Corinth for one of these events.

To make the games "happen," there was a city official, elected annually, called the "gymnasiarch." Funding for the games came from wealthy citizens who were asked to sponsor a particular year's event. We don't know whether there was an admission fee to attend the games, but admission would not

Mosaic floor from office of the Director of the Isthmian
Games. The victorious athlete, palm in hand and crowned
with a wreath of withered celery, stands before the Goddess
of Good Fortune, thanking her for his success.
(From Broneer, p. 93.)

fund the entire event. Incidentally, grounds-keeping was the
responsibility of the contestants.[10] The office of the manager of
the Isthimean Games has been identified on the Bema in Corinth.

In spite of the fact that the games were always religious
events, St. Paul saw the opportunity to use them as a metaphor
for the Gospel (I Cor. 9:24). The metaphor of running a race is
not uncommon in the Bible, and St. Paul, himself, uses this
metaphor in other letters, but this is the only place where he
makes reference to the prize, and it is clear that he is addressing
the sports mania in Corinth, where one of the four "crown"
games was held.

St. Paul has sometimes been characterized as being at least a minor sports fanatic, but he clearly doesn't think competing in sports is more important than anything else. Part of the reason circumcision was an issue was its relevance to sports. Sports were conducted in the nude, and a circumcised man was prohibited from competition. Josephus tells about Jewish males who "concealed their circumcision" in order to compete.[11] The Talmud makes explicit reference to Hellenizing Jews who had surgery to reverse their circumcision.[12] So, when St. Paul says to the Corinthians that they should not change their status regarding circumcision: "Let him not seek to remove the marks of circumcision . . . Let him not seek circumcision." (I Cor. 7:18), he is talking partly about the Jewish covenant, but also partly about the Isthmian Games.

In our own day, we sometimes wonder if sports have taken over our world. No more so than in St. Paul's day.

---

1 Golden, p. 72. See also Mary Renault's description of a wrestling match at the Isthmian games in her novel, *The Last of the Wine*, pp. 169-173.

2 Robinson, p. 209. For a discussion of the value of a talent, see the essay, "Public and Private Money."

3 Robinson, p. 205.

4 Harris, 1964, p. 159. Mary Renault describes the crowd at the Olympic games in her novel, *The Mask of Apollo,* ch. XVII, pp. 278-284.

5 Golden, p. 61.

6 Harris, 1976, pp. 36-37.

7 Golden, pp. 40-42.

8 Harris, 1964, p. 37.

9 Golden, pp. 55-57.

10 Harris, 1964, pp. 151-156.

11 Josephus A.J. 12.241 – quoted by Sweet, p. 133.

12 *Talmud Shabbath* 19.2 – Quoted by Sweet, p. 133.

WILD ANIMALS IN THE CITY

From our own experience we know that popular tastes in entertainment change over time. For example, the most popular television programs will at one time be scripted dramas, and at another time the most popular will be "talent" programs. The same thing was true in ancient Greece and Rome. Every major city in the Greek world had a theatre, usually dedicated to the god Dionysus, where elaborate dramas were staged. Literature students still study the scripts that have survived, written by Aeschylus, Sophocles, Euripides, Aristophanes, and others. Many of these plays required what modern motion picture producers call "special effects," and these elaborate effects are engagingly described in Mary Renault's novel, *The Mask of Apollo*, set 400 years before St. Paul.[1] The novel tells us about professional actors who traveled all over the Greek world. By the time of St. Paul, public tastes in entertainment had changed.[2] The 21st Century visitor will find two theatres next to each other a little West of the Temple of Apollo, but the smaller of the two, the Odeion, was apparently built three or four decades after St. Paul visited the city, so he knew only the large theatre, which had lasted for four centuries. It had been built for dramas and political assemblies, but was now used for animal spectacles. In fact, apparently because much of the population that Julius Caesar brought into the city when he restored it was non-Greek, Corinth was the Greek city with the best known animal shows. Writers of the era complain that cities such as Athens were seeking to emulate the worst of Corinth by bringing animal shows into their theatres.

We can see the evidence of these shows in what remains of the ancient theatre. The Romans removed the ten lowest rows of seats to make the arena floor that we can see today, and a nine-foot wall with an iron grating on top was erected to protect the spectators from animals getting loose within the audience.

This was not yet the era of Christians being thrown to the lions. The animal shows were, at first, hunting exhibitions. As crowds tired of the predictability of hunting shows, various things were done to keep the public entertained, and at some point it became customary to execute condemned criminals by tying them up and letting animals attack them. Apuleius tells a story about a woman who was found guilty of several murders, and was condemned to be the focus of a show, first by having sexual relations with a donkey, and then being torn apart by carnivorous beasts.[3] Apuleius was writing to entertain, but the story is probably based on a certain amount of reality.

The next escalation in the shows was gladiatorial combat, although we don't know for sure whether gladiators fought to the death while St. Paul was in the city.

By the end of the century, the animal shows had been moved to another venue, and the Theatre once again hosted plays and public meetings.

A number of paintings representing the animal shows have been found on the walls in the Theater, including depictions of people killing animals and gymnasts vaulting over attacking animals. One of the paintings is apparently a depiction of the story of Androcles, who is said to have removed a thorn from the paw of a wild lion, then later was forced to face that same lion in the arena. The lion refused to attack him.[4] In later versions of this legend, Androcles is seen as a Christian who is then freed. Playwright George Bernard Shaw used this legend memorably in his 1913 dark comedy, "Androcles and the Lion," a play which he claimed was more against the British Empire than against the Roman Empire.[5] The play concludes not only with Androcles receiving his freedom, but with the lion intimidating everyone in sight. At the end of the drama Androcles says, "Come, Tommy. Whilst we stand together, no cage for you, no slavery for me." (He goes out with the lion, everybody crowding away to give him as wide a berth as possible.)

St. Paul writes about having fought "wild beasts" in Ephesus (I Cor. 15:32), and probably means this as a metaphor because (a) he was a Roman citizen, and citizens were not subject to such punishment, (b) if he had fought, he would have mentioned it in II Cor 11:23-29, and (c) if he had fought, Acts would have reported the miracle of his escape. So he didn't really fight "wild beasts," but the members of the Corinthian congregation knew what he was talking about. Most of them had probably seen one or more animal shows at the Theatre.

---

[1] Renault, Mary. *The Mask of Apollo*, 1966.

[2] Most of the information in this article comes from Capps.

[3] Apuleius, pp. 229-234.

[4] McDonald, p. 45.

[5] Shaw.

GITY OF TEMPLES

The ancient city of Corinth died as a result of a series of disasters over several centuries.[1] In 395 the Goths attacked and burned it. This led to a plumbing problem: the Roman storm sewers no longer functioned, so debris accumulated on the site of the city. People rebuilt, but in 521 an earthquake devastated the area. Once again they rebuilt, and it was a sustainable community, but never again the great city of classical times. The ruins of the classical city remained buried for more than a thousand years. In 1858, there was another major earthquake, and the residents of "Old Corinth" abandoned the site and built the "New Corinth" that today we find on the gulf a few miles from the ancient ruins.[2] In 1896, the Greek government granted permission to the American School of Classical Studies to excavate the ancient city, and studies of ancient Corinth have now gone on for more than a hundred years.

Throughout the centuries, no matter what has happened on the site of ancient Corinth, there has been one constant: the Temple of Apollo. This temple, constructed six-hundred years before Christ, dominated the classical city of Greek and Roman times, survived earthquakes and fire, and stood as the only indication of the grandeur of the ancient city until we began uncovering the ruins in 1896. Today we can visit the ancient ruins and see how the Temple of Apollo was something everybody saw every day. Like the courthouse on the square in many U.S. county seat towns, the temple was something you were always aware of, even if you seldom or never visited it. But we can also see in a 1905 photograph how this temple was an indelible mark on the wasteland that had once been a grand city.

The ruins of ancient Corinth in 1905. Notice that the Temple of Apollo is the only thing visible. All other ruins had been covered by several feet of dirt and debris, so no one knew what might lie underneath. (From West, p. 393.)

We get the sense that when St. Paul visited the city, Apollo was no longer a major god in the minds of the people. The patron goddess of the city was Aphrodite, whose statue stood "armed"on the summit of the Acrocorinth, and whose servants, according to rumor and legend, worked to satisfy the sexual urges of tourists.[3] The local population seems to have favored the "mystery religions" of Demeter, Dionysus and Isis.

As a matter of fact, St. Paul visited a city that was full of temples, and more were under construction during the eighteen months he was there. Even so, because of its massive presence, the Temple of Apollo was a major symbol of the city.

Apollo was at the center of Greek mythology. A son of Zeus, he inherited Zeus' seemingly insatiable lust for beautiful mortal women, and among his children by various women were Orpheus, the musician and Asclepius, the healer. Apollo's godly duties included poetry and music, healing, prophecy, and keeping the sun in its course. He was a god of many names, and he was called Helios when he took care of the sun. A statue of Apollo as Helios (or Helius) joined the statue of Aphrodite on the summit of the Acrocorinth.

Without exception, the Greek gods and goddesses were vain and short-tempered,[4] and Apollo especially showed his temper when anyone challenged his musical preeminence. One story is that Apollo had a musical contest with Pan, and Apollo won, of course, but King Midas (of "golden touch" fame) claimed that Apollo had won unfairly. Apollo responded by transforming Midas' ears into those of a donkey. Another version says that Midas, serving as judge, awarded the prize to Pan, whereupon Apollo gave Midas the donkey ears.

Another time, a satyr named Marsyas challenged Apollo to a musical contest, the terms being that the winner could do absolutely anything to the loser. Marsyas lost. Consequently, according to the terms of the bet, Apollo skinned Marsyas alive.[5] The result of this gruesome contest was that Corinth got the flute, which was deposited in the Corinthian Temple of Apollo,[6] although the smaller town of Sicyon, seven miles northwest of Corinth also claimed the flute.

The traveler Pausanias, writing a hundred years after St. Paul's visit, said that the flute had been destroyed in a fire.[7]

This was a story of godly vanity that led to a cruel murder. How conscious of this story were the people of Corinth? We have no way of knowing, but there may have been at least some subliminal reminder whenever they saw the ancient temple. If so, the teaching of St. Paul was a shocking alternative: "In Christ, God was reconciling the world to himself, not counting their trespasses against them, and entrusting the message of reconciliation to us." (II Cor. 5:19). Some authors claim that Christ is just another of the many names for Apollo, but St. Paul denied this, saying that Christ was not vain, and Christ was not petty. Christ, who "died for all," would not murder someone out of vanity.

Then there are the temples. We're not sure how many there were when St. Paul visited the city, but there were a lot of them. The members of the congregation could not help thinking of all these temples when they heard St. Paul's words:
". . . do you not know that your body is a temple of the Holy Spirit within you, which you have from God, and that you are not your own? For you were bought with a price, therefore glorify God in your body." (I Cor. 6:19-20.)
"For we are the temple of the living God; as God said, 'I will live in them and walk among them, and I will be their God, and they shall be my people.'" (II Cor. 6:16.)

1 Weinberg and Weinberg.

2 A contemporary traveler had this to say about it: "But, a truly over-whelming disaster befell Corinth, in the earthquake of last February; and the place now presents a woeful scene of desolation. Some of the houses have been leveled to the ground, but all have been rendered uninhabitable, and the whole population are living in tents. The de-structive shock fortunately occurred at 10 a.am, so that many were out of doors. In a town so small, the loss of life was slight, compared to what we hear of in populous countries: nevertheless sixteen or eight-een people were killed . . . and several much hurt." Wyse, pp. 315-316.

3 The Corinthian horde of prostitutes may have been mostly legen-dary. See the essay, "Aphrodite and Her Girls."

4 Marie Phillips has written an amusing, although somewhat "raw" novel about the Greek gods titled *Gods Behaving Badly*. The premise is that the gods have fallen on hard times, and are living together in a run-down house in London. Their vanity and sense of entitlement is a central feature of the plot.

5 For details of this myth, see the Introduction.

6 Olalla, p. 65.

7 Pausanias, p. 287.

Aphrodite

APHRODITE AND HER GIRLS

Strabo visited Corinth 75 or 80 years before St. Paul's visit, and wrote in his influential book about Greece:

> Corinth is called wealthy because of its commerce, since it is situated on the Isthmus and is master of two harbours. . . . The temple of Aphrodite was so rich that it owned more than a thousand temple-slaves, courtesans, whom both men and women had dedicated to the goddess. And therefore it was also on account of these women that the city was crowded with people and grew rich; for instance, the ship-captains freely squandered their money, and hence the proverb, "Not for every man is the voyage to Corinth."[1]

Most seminary students who take a course in the Corinthian letters will know about Strabo's report of 1,000 temple prostitutes, even if they have never read Strabo, or even know who he was. The essence of the report sounds reasonable, even if the number was far fewer than 1,000, because Corinth was a major port of call, and everyone "knows" about sailors. Everyone also "knows" about Aphrodite, the goddess of "love," and that the statue of Aphrodite watched over the city from the top of the Acrocorinth.

What, then, did Aphrodite mean for St. Paul and his congregation? The answer depends a lot on the facts. How big a business was prostitution in Corinth? How visible was it in the culture of Corinth?

Surprisingly, we have little archeological evidence about Corinthian prostitution. If you visit the ruins of ancient Ephesus, the guide will be sure to tell you about the tunnel under a main street that allowed men to visit a house of prostitution without being seen, and in the excavation of Pompeii we can see the ruins of a floor plan that could be nothing other than a place of prostitution, but there's nothing like that in ancient Corinth. Also, in Corinth we have not uncovered a building with "bawdy" mosaics or frescoes that might indicate the building was used as a house of ill-fame.

We don't know much about the temple of Aphrodite on the summit of the Acrocorinth, but nothing we know indicates that in any era the temple grounds provided space for prostitution, and the temple in the center of the city was pretty small. No space there for 100 girls, much less 1,000. The closest we come to evidence is found in the theatre. An inscription from the time of Euripides and Aristophanes says, "Belonging to the Girls."[2] Respectable women did not attend theatre (all roles, male and female, were played by men), but there was evidently space reserved for some women at the theatre. Who were they, if not Aphrodite's "girls?"

Corinthian coin from the time of
Emperor L. Verus (co-emperor with
Marcus Aurelius): Aphrodie, naked
to the waist, looking at a shield.
Eros is handing her something,
perhaps a ribbon.
This coin is apparently based on
the statue on the Acrocorinth after
the reestablishment of the city.
(Imhoof-Blumer and Gardner, plate
G, coin CXXII. See pp. 25-26.)

No doubt we're missing something. There is a lot of Corinth that has not been excavated. For example, we have not found a synagogue, but there must have been several. So we also have not found a house of prostitution, even though they surely existed. Wherever they were, they were not "right down town" as part of the establishment. The director of the Isthemean Games had an office "down town,"[3] but not the priest or priestess who might have supervised Aphrodite's "girls." Where does this lead us? Hopefully to a more realistic and "rounded" view of life in Corinth. Some people have characterized the city as one vast house of prostitution, and if that were so, there would be little connection we could make between our daily life and daily life in ancient Corinth. If sexual activity was carried out indiscriminately everywhere, or if half-nude prostitutes were advertising their services in the market-place and everywhere else,[4] then the culture of Corinth would be so radically different from ours that we would be able to discount what St. Paul writes about prostitutes as being applicable only to places where no one had any sense of modesty or morality.

In fact, our culture may be more sexual than that of ancient Corinth, given our ubiquitous strip-clubs, the sexually suggestive advertisements in shopping malls and "family" publications, and everywhere else.

No matter what the situation may have been in Strabo's time, after Augustus imposed Roman morality on the empire, prostitution was certainly not a "downtown" business. Of course prostitution existed, and there were lots of travelers to take advantage of it, but prostitution was not sponsored by state -approved temples, even temples of Aphrodite.[5] These things, however are never simple. Aphrodite was still the goddess in charge of love.

On top of the Acrocorinth, Aphrodite was either a warrior, or a lady coming out of the bath. She seems to have been remembered as a warrior, but in St. Paul's time, the statue was a lady who had finished bathing. Imhoof-Blumer and Gardner say that that statue was "new" in Roman times.[6] At the Acrocorinth temple, she was served by a matron who was to be chaste during her term of service and by a virgin "Bath-bearer" who was to serve in her virginity for a year.[7] In the downtown Agora or Forum she was also respectable.

Where, then, is the lascivious goddess of "love?" Archeologists may have found her next to the theatre. Let's think about the theatre. In classical Greece, about 450 years before St. Paul, it was common to see plays produced that featured fairly explicit sexual references, often for comic effect. We have no reason to think that such plays were not still being produced for mass audiences in the Roman era. Of course, in the Roman era, the theatre also became the site for animal shows and gladiatorial combat, which eventually took priority over drama, but any public entertainment provides an opportunity for prostitutes to sell their services, so it might not be surprising to find prostitutes looking for customers in the area of the theatre.

As we have already noted, apparently the "girls" had a reserved section in the theatre several hundred years before St. Paul. Likewise in the Roman era, when St. Paul visited the city, Aphrodite had a presence near the theatre. Archeologists have found part of a nude statue of the goddess nearby. (Apparently it was destroyed in later centuries by Christians who wanted to clean up remnants of paganism.) Charles K. Williams II, recent director of Corinth excavation, has written, "one can deduce that Aphrodite was an important presence in the area east of the theater in the first and second centuries C.E.,"[8] but then Williams cautions that we still have no evidence of a house of prostitution, and he suggests that even though we might see this statue and related material as "bawdy," the cult centered near the theatre *might* be related to family and procreation. Maybe Aphrodite near the theatre was a wholesome family girl, or maybe she had resumed her character as patroness of sexuality.

Whatever the case, there was no "sacred" prostitution at the theatre. In other words, there wasn't a "sacrament" of sexuality there as part of the worship of Aphrodite. But there was prostitution. It is likely that prostitutes prayed especially to Aphrodite, and "common sense" suggests that prostitutes might have sought a blessing from the nude Aphrodite of the theatre. In the congregation established by St. Paul there was someone who wanted to defend the practice of visiting prostitutes. We can never know the exact situation, but St. Paul was clearly reacting to something specific in the congregation in I Cor. 6:13-20. Some people have suggested that St. Paul's argument against prostitution was actually a reaction against association with the pagan goddess,[9] but it seems likely that it was also a general reaction against purchasing the services of prostitutes no matter what their religion may have been. This is his basic attitude in I Thess. 4:3. If so, it also applies to us.[10]

---

[1] Strabo, *Geography*, 8.6.20, quoted by Lanci. Lanci's article has provided much background for this essay.

[2] McDonald, p. 46.

[3] Broneer, p. 93. We reproduce the picture of the office floor mosaic on p. 80 in this book.

[4] This is the situation imagined in the middle of the 1800s by novelist Alexandre Dumas (of *Three Musketeers* fame), who had a character in a novel about Roman Corinth say, "Corinth is the city of courtesans . . . we fear so much that we should fail in our supply, that we cause them to be purchased in Byzantium, in the isles of the Archipelago, and in Sicily. They are recognized by their unveiled faces and bare bosoms." The character went on to explain that other women always veiled themselves in public for fear of being thought "a votary of Venus." — Dumas, p. 12.

[5] Budin reviewed the evidence and concluded that even though there has been prostitution, there has never been "sacred prostitution." All accounts of so-called "sacred prostitution" speak of events far distant and far back in time from the time and place of the author. Budin,   pp. 90-91.

[6] Imhoof-Blumer and Gardner, pp. 25-26.

[7] Bookidis and Stroud, p. 301.

8 Williams, pp. 243-247.

9 Rosner gives a good review of these arguments and those scholars who conclude that the issue is "sacred" prostitution. Rosner himself argues that St. Paul's issue is not "sacred" prostitution, but prostitutes who sell their services at various festivals. "Common sense" suggests that Rosner's proposal may be "correct," but too limited. Wouldn't St. Paul's instruction relate to prostitution wherever it is practiced?

10 In the U.S., prostitution is legal in Nye County, Nevada, and in 2010 this led to a moral dilemma, because the county was depending on revenue from prostitute licenses. Faced with an over-all revenue shortfall, the county had to consider raising the price of prostitute licenses, and then promoting prostitution in order to provide necessary revenue for the county. (*Army Times*, Apr. 19,2010, p. 3.)

The road leaving the Theatre area.

SEX IN THE CITY

Was the culture of Roman Corinth any more erotically charged than the culture of early 21st Century USA? Perhaps not. Perhaps the things that St. Paul said about sexuality to the congregation in Roman Corinth apply directly to the congregations of our time. Ancient Corinth was sexually charged, with pornography readily available, common prostitution, homosexuality and bisexuality considered normal, risqué dramatic productions . . . and how is all of this different from our time? A concern with sexuality pervades the first letter to the Corinthians. We find it in chapter 5, chapter 7, chapter 10, and then in chapter 11, on a different note, we have the question of the role of women in the church. As we have seen elsewhere,[1] Corinth had a reputation for sexual license, and although the reputation was probably overstated, it no doubt had a basis in fact. We also know that in classical Greece (300-400 years prior to St. Paul) sexuality was spoken of and celebrated quite openly in the theatre, in poetry, in vase paintings,[2] and in the writings of the philosophers. It was not a Victorian era.

During the reign of Caesar Augustus, there was an official attempt to put a lid on sexual license throughout the Empire. Both men and women of child bearing age were given various inducements to marry, bachelors were limited in the inheritance they could receive, and widowed and divorced women were required to remarry within a specified time. Divorce was made more difficult than it had been before. Homosexuality was out-lawed.[3]

One might say that the theme of I Corinthians is, "Don't be arrogant." In spite of the imperial law, St. Paul saw members of the congregation acting arrogantly through the practice of sexual immorality. While the imperial law was effective in some areas, it may have been less effective in Greece, especially a Greek seaport city such as Corinth. We can take I Corinthians as evidence that there was sexual license in the Corinth to which St. Paul was writing. None of his other letters emphasize sexuality the way this one does, and it seems likely that if sexual license was evident in the congregation it would have been evident throughout the city.

Let's turn the clock back and look at a drama by Euripides called *Hippolytus*. Even though it was several hundred years old by the time of St. Paul, it was by one of the Greek's greatest playwrights, and would have been known. Indeed, the Roman poet Ovid, who died about the time St. Paul was born, wrote a version of "Hippolytus," defending hedonism.[4] The major characters, for our purposes, are the goddess Aphrodite, a young man named Hippolytus, and the young man's step-mother, Phaedra. Hippolytus chose to worship Artemis, the chaste goddess of the hunt, and consequently chooses a life of chastity.

This choice was an affront to Aphrodite, the goddess of love and procreation, and she decided to punish Hippolytus. She did this by causing Pheadra to have an insane lust for her step-son, a lust which Hippolytus spurned. The tragedy reached a climax with the rejected Phaedra committing suicide, leaving behind a note accusing Hippolytus of having raped her.

The obvious moral is that no good can come from dishonoring Aphrodite, and this would be especially true in Corinth, which acknowledged and worshipped a (possibly) military Aphrodite who might even use the weapons of war against anyone who dishonored her. Beyond this, Aphrodite, who had been born from the sea, was almost as effective as Poisidon when it came to controlling the angry waves, so sailors who came into Corinth would be well advised to worship at both temples.

If a critic responds that the myth of Pheadra is simply fiction, we can turn to the fact that men desiring their stepmothers was a common cultural theme at this time. Pinault gives us a lengthy analysis of these cases, including an account relating that a physician discovered that a young man who appeared to be near death was actually love-sick for his father's new wife. When the physician explained the "illness" to the father, he readily gave the woman to his son.[5]

Might all of this have something to do with I Cor. 5:1? St. Paul says, "It is actually reported that there is sexual immorality among you, and of a kind that is not found even among pagans; for a man is living with his father's wife." There has been much speculation about the matter St. Paul is referring to, and it is nothing but speculation, but certainly the "father's wife" could have been a "step mother" closer to the son's age than to the father's age, a "Phaedra" with a "Hipploytus." It is unlikely that anyone would have used Euripides' drama or the underlying mythology to justify whatever was going on, but the drama was part of the cultural background, and might have played a "subconscious" role in making the activity "all right."[6]

In the last couple of decades, we have seen a great increase in the number of women who pursue classical scholarship, and this has led to many published studies of the structure of families in classical Greece with an emphasis on the place of women in the family. At this time, there is no consensus about the role of women. Some say that they had almost no freedom, others say that they did have freedom.[7]

The notion that women did not have freedom is reinforced by a well known quotation attributed to the orator Demosthenes: "We have *hetairai* for pleasure, concubines for our day-to-day physical well-being, and wives in order to beget legitimate children and have trustworthy guardians of our households."[8] The context for this quotation is a lawsuit which Demosthenes is prosecuting against a woman named Neaira. She is claiming to be a legitimate citizen of Athens and a wife of a citizen. She is accused of having been a prostitute in Corinth before moving to Athens, of attending drinking parties with men, with prostituting herself in Athens and charging high prices because she was a "citizen-wife." Meanwhile her husband was accused of blackmailing Neaira's customers. The prosecution claimed that all of this meant that Neaira was neither a legitimate wife nor a citizen.[9]

The details of the case against Neaira are not relevant to our concern, because con-artists and loose women are a fact of life at all times and in all places.[10] The point is that Demosthenes assumed that normal (male) jurors would agree that *hetairai* (high priced prostitutes) and concubines were a normal part of society, and that wives (the result of arranged marriages) were simply a way to get heirs.

Society may have changed between the time of Demosthenes and the time of St. Paul, and wives may have been more loved and appreciated by their husbands in Roman Corinth than in classical Corinth. Even so, there were probably men in Roman Corinth who would agree with the sentiment Demosthenes expressed. There are also men in our time who agree with this sentiment. This common male view provides the context for St. Paul's long statement about husbands and wives being faithful to one another (I Cor. 6:12-7:40).

---

1 See the essay, "Aphrodite and Her Girls."

2 Neils gives accurate verbal descriptions of such scenes.

3 Ferguson, p. 69.

4 Ovid, says on p. 38, "Jupiter has determined that whatever is pleasing, the same is pious." Note that Ovid was exiled from Rome, ostensibly because of his sexually provocative writing.

5 Pinault, pp. 62-68.

6 St. Paul's comment about pagans not doing it may be drawn from another well known drama, *Oedipus Rex* by Sophocles.

7 Cline, in an article written several decades ago, gives a useful review of the scholarly debate that will certainly continue for several decades to come, p. 183, footnote 2.

8 Dover, p. 14.

9 Thornton, pp. 165-166.

10 We say more about prostitution in Corinth in the essay, "Aphrodite and Her Girls."

THE ANCIENT HOSPITAL

As far as we know, there were two primary places of healing in Corinth at the time of St. Paul: on the Acrocorinth, the temple to Sarapis Canopus[1] and the temple of Asclepius, which was the main "hospital." We don't know anything about healing activities at the Sarapis temple, although this temple, a "newcomer" on the scene, might have been seen as "alternative medicine" analogous to the variety of "alternative" treatments available today to those who, for whatever reason, don't trust their medical doctor.

The difference is that in St. Paul's time, the chief medical practitioners seem to have been pagan priests who would supervise the rites of their cult. This is not to say that medicine was unknown. Hippocrates of Cos (a Greek island), known today as the "father of medicine," was active about 450 years before St. Paul. He claimed to be a direct descendant (17 generations removed) of Aesculapius, as well as a descendent of Hercules, but he did not claim priestly powers. Instead he depended on observation and his doctrines influenced medicine for a couple of thousand years.[2] In addition, about two generations after Hippocrates, a medical school was established at Alexandria, Egypt, that made empirical studies of anatomy. Even dissection may have been done at Alexandria. A century *after* St. Paul, Galen dissected animals for medical knowledge, and may have dissected human cadavars.[3] St. Paul lived during a peak in the advance of medical knowledge, all of which was available throughout the Roman Empire, but we don't have evidence of organized centers of healing other than the temples.

Asclepius was an illegitimate child of the god Apollo. His mother, a mortal, while still pregnant with the child, forsook the god for a mortal lover. Apollo, very upset at being jilted, killed her, but rescued the unborn baby and asked the centaur, Chiron, to raise him. The child grew up to become known as a skilled healer, so skilled that he once accepted payment to bring a dead man back to life. Zeus couldn't allow this, so he killed Asclepius.[4] In the course of things, Asclepius became a god, with responsibility for healing, and temples were erected to him throughout Greece.

We can tell when a statue, picture, or coin is supposed to represent Asclepius, because he is inevitably accompanied by snakes. Some say that the medical caduceus came from Asclepius, although others claim that the staff of Asclepius had only one snake, while the staff of Hermes, messenger of the gods, had two snakes[5] (although the single snake staff might be traced to the Old Testament, Numbers 21:8, and others tie the caduceus to the worship of Dionysus).[6]

The Corinthian Temple of Asclepius was constructed near a spring about a quarter of a mile north of the market area, not too far from the Lechaeum Road, one of the main roads out of the city. The ancient poet Pindar praised the healing powers of the god: "All those who came to him with ulcerous sores, with limbs wounded by grisly bronze or far-thrown stones and with bodies ravaged by summer fever or wintery cold, each one he delivered from his special pain, treating some with soothing spells, some with healthful potions or spreading on their limbs ointments from far and near, or making them right again with the knife."[7]

Our best information about the healing rites comes from a comedy drama by Aristophanes called *Plutus*. In this play, Wealth (personified) who is blind, seeks treatment. The specified treatment is in several stages: (1) a bath in the sea, (2) additional cleansing at a water basin, (3) cleansing the mind so that one thinks only pure thoughts when entering the temple, (4) offering honey-cakes at the altar, (5) another cleansing, (6) enter the main hall and lie down on a pallet on the floor, (7) sleep, encouraged by an attendant, (8) a dream in which the god and an attendant apply a healing plaster which is then licked off by a sacred snake.[8]

When we read about the form of "treatment" offered in the temple, we must wonder if the priests might have been familiar with some of the writings of Hippocrates, especially his comment that "Nature is sufficient of itself for every animal. She performs everything that is necessary to them without any instruction how to do it. She distributes the blood, spirits and heat through all parts of the body, by which means it receives life and sensation, nourishment, preservation and growth."[9] In other words, if you don't know what to do to assist in healing, leave it alone and see if nature takes care of it.

Ceramic body parts left at the Temple of Asclepius. (From Broneer, p. 83.)

All of the apostles seem, at one time or another, to have claimed the spiritual gift of healing, but we have no record of St. Paul praying for the healing of anyone during his stay in Corinth in spite of the fact that in his first letter he mentions healing as being a true gift of the Spirit (I Cor. 12:9). According to Acts 19: 11-12, he did facilitate healing during his stay in Ephesus. Why, then, is there no record of his working to heal anyone in Corinth? We don't know.

Maybe the Temple of Asclepius provides an unexpected link to St. Paul's work in Corinth. As a thank offering for healing at the Temple of Asclepius, the Corinthian patients often left behind plaster replicas of the healed body-part. Archaeologists excavating the Temple have found enough of these life-size models of arms, legs, feet, hands, heads, eyes, ears, breasts and genitals to fill a box 30 feet by 30 feet by 30 feet.[10] A representative sample of thesebody parts is on display in the Corinth museum.

When he wrote to the congregation at Corinth, St. Paul gave a long discourse on the congregation as a "body" in which all must work together, each contributing the particular skills that God has given (I Cor. 12:14-25). This passage has attracted the interest of biblical scholars who wonder why he selected this "body" image to speak to the disunity in the congregation. He mentioned this "body" metaphor in Romans, Ephesians and Colossians, but it is only in the letter to the Corinthians that he extends his discussion of the metaphor. Why?

Scholars have argued that St. Paul borrowed the metaphor from Greek philosophy, or from the Old Testament, or from Gnosticism. Maybe so, but maybe he thought about the useless plaster body parts in the Corinthian temple of Asclepius, and thus developed his metaphor.[11] Certainly, no matter why this "body" metaphor came to St. Paul, the members of the Corinthian congregation would have thought about the temple of Asclepius.

---

1 Smith, pp. 227-228.

2 Greenhill, p. 483.

3 Greenhill, p. 213.

4 Pindar tells us this story.

5 Wallraff, p. 154.

6 Euripides, *The Bacchae*, describing the staff of Dionysus: "Then a horned god was found, and a god of serpents crowned; and for that are serpents wound in the wands his maidens bear," p. 353.

7 Quoted by Lang, p. 6.

8 See Aristophenes, *Plutus*, act III, scene II (650-708).

9 Smythe, p. 33.

10 Lang, p. 15.

11 Hill, Andrew E., pp. 437-439.

A MYSTERY IS NOT A
—WHODUNIT—

Around the time of Alexander the Great, as loyalty to the old gods of the Greek pantheon waned, several new cults, which we have come to call "mystery religions" became important. Although each of these cults had special specific teachings, and although each varied somewhat from site to site, they shared several characteristics. One characteristic was secrecy, which explains why we call them "*mystery* religions."
The vow of secrecy had to do with the specific initiation rituals and ceremonies, and initiates took their vows seriously, so we don't know much specific about the cult ceremonies or forms of worship. In spite of this, we know quite a bit about the beliefs and teachings of these cults. The "mystery religions" all dealt with death and the underworld as related to the change of seasons. Those who were initiated were assured of "salvation" (*soteria*), meaning a good life after death.

In Corinth, there were strong groups worshipping the mysteries of Demeter, Isis, and Dionysus. In addition, the ancient cult of Aphrodite may have developed some "mystery" characteristics. The myths of Demeter (an old Greek goddess) and Isis (an old Egyptian goddess) both have to do with contesting and bargaining with death and, in some sense, winning the contest. The myth of Dionysus, in its oldest form, does not relate to death, but in its mystery form, the myth of Dionysus included a defeat of death. From earliest times, Demeter and Dionysus had to do with the fertility of the earth, and the European version of Isis became a fertility goddess, sometimes conflated with the fertility goddess, Aphrodite. (Another widespread mystery religion, that of Mithra, does not seem to have been a force in Corinth.)

The evidence we have about the nature of mystery worship indicates that in each of the "mystery religions," the initiation ritual consisted of dramatic reenactment of the cult's story. Much of this evidence comes from paintings, sculpture, and study of the archeological remains of sanctuaries. The most extensive ancient description of mystery ceremony is found at the end of an ancient "novel," *The Golden Ass* by Apuleius. In the thirteenth book (or chapter) the hero of the novel, Lucius, who has been changed into a donkey and gone through many adventures, prays to the goddess of many names to be changed back to a man. The goddess comes to him in a dream, reveals her real name as Isis, and instructs him as to what he should do. His transformation back into human form takes place during the great Isis-cult procession at Cenchreae, one of the ports of Corinth. The ceremony is a public procession celebrating the coming of spring, not a secret initiation. In the novel, Lucius then is initiated, and he discovers that it costs a lot of money to join the cult. Not only that, but when he moves from Corinth to Rome, he has to spend even more money to be initiated into the Roman chapter of the club.[1]

The words are *mysterion*, meaning "mystery" or "secret," and *myeo*, meaning "to be initiated" or "to learn the secret."

St. Paul uses the word *mysterion* in I Cor. 1:23, where the NRSV translates it as "foolishness," and 2:1 (NRSV: "mystery") and 7 (NRSV: "secret). Bornkamm comments that, in St. Paul's writings, "The *mysterion* is the eternal counsel of God which is hidden from the world but eschatologically fulfilled in the cross of the Lord of glory and which carries with it the glorification of believers. . . . The *mysterion* is not itself revelation; it is the object of revelation."[2] Robertson and Plummer, in their classic commentary say, regarding 2:7, "The 'wisdom' is [a mystery], because it has been for so long a secret, although now made known to all who can receive it."[3] This is precisely what St. Paul says in Rom. 16:25-26. In other words, at the beginning of I Cor., St. Paul uses the word "mystery" to refer to a truth that is different from the "truth" that initiates learn when they join a cult, but he is making a connection with those who are familiar with mystery religions.[4] Barclay explains that for the Corinthians, "mystery," as a technical religious term, refers to a ceremony "whose meaning was quite clear to the members of the society, but unintelligible to the outsider. What Paul is saying is, 'We go on to explain things which only the man who has already given his heart to Christ can understand.'"[5] This is what it means for St. Paul to say that he and the other apostles are "stewards of God's mysteries." (I Cor. 4:1)

In addition to being a ceremony, the "mystery" was a story: the story of how the goddess or god overcame problems and even overcame the guardian of Hades. The message St. Paul preached was also a story: the story of how the Son of God was born as a human, lived with us, taught us, was executed, raised from the dead, ascended into heaven, and will come again. The purpose of all of this was to reconcile the population of the entire world as a peaceful new humanity. He says this explicitly in Ephesians 2:11-22, and proceeds to explain in the next paragraph, Ephesians 3:1-6. The NRSV translation committee decided, with good reason, to translate the word "it" as "mystery" in Ephesians 3:5.

Incidentally, to see that St. Paul was indeed aware of the connections he was making by using this technical religious word, refer to Philippians 4:12, "I know what it is to have little, and I know what it is to have plenty. In any and all circumstances I have learned the *secret* of being well-fed and of going hungry, of having plenty and of being in need." The word translated "secret" is a form of *myeo*, the technical word for initiation into the mysteries. This is the only occurrence of this word in the New Testament, and Bornkamm sees it as "an ironical echo of the mysteries." In other words, St. Paul is making a slight joke that his daily life is an initiation into the mysteries of God.[6]

While this word was primarily used as a technical religious term, Plato also used the word *mysterion* in his philosophy, not applying it to secret rituals, but as a way of explaining that philosophical truth is hidden from those who see only the external world. A person must devote studious energy to understand the mystery of philosophical truth. So in the opening of First Corinthians, St. Paul not only connected with those for whom mystery religions were an existential reality, but also with the "wise" elite who were above the common crowd and their cults, and he made the point that the wisdom of God is not the wisdom of Plato, the "mystery" of God is not the mystery of Plato.

So, by the use of one word, St. Paul is saying that faith in Christ is better than the secret cults and better than the exalted teaching of the philosophers.

Later in the letter, I Cor. 13:2, St. Paul says that it is of no use to understand "all mysteries." Here the reference would not be to the special "mystery of God," but explicitly to the mystery religions. If a person had enough money and time, it would be possible to become an initiate in every one of the secret cults. They were not exclusive. However St. Paul says to the faithful, "Don't bother."

In I Cor. 14:2, St. Paul pursues one of the primary themes of his letter, that we should live for one another, not live for ourselves. He refers to a person who prays in tongues, and says that such "mysteries" do no good for anyone other than the one who prays. Doing good for yourself is not the best use of prayer.

At the end of his long discussion of resurrection, I Cor. 15:51, St. Paul exclaims, "Lo, I tell you a mystery!" Here he does not seem to be trying to teach in the way he was earlier in the letter, but in his excitement as he dictates the letter, he "grabs" the first word that comes to mind, and, given his earlier use of the word, it is well said.

---

[1] Apuleius, pp. 235-255.

[2] Bornkamm, p. 617.

3 Robertson and Plummer, p. 37.

4 There are commentators who insist that St. Paul's use of the word has nothing to do with the "mystery religions." (For example, Barth, pp. 123-127.) Certainly the "mystery" of Jesus Christ is different from that of the "mystery religions," but when the people of Corinth heard the word "mystery," they would have immediately related it to the "mystery religions." We have to think that St. Paul was using the analogy intentionally. The simple difference between faith in Jesus and faith in a "mystery" is (1) the secret is not "secret," (2) "initiation" does not cost anything, and (3) the religion of Jesus is hopeful with far greater rewards than the pessimistic "mystery religions."

5 Barclay, p. 26.

6 Bornkamm, p. 619.

MYSTERIES ON THE MOUNTAIN

The ancient city was on relatively flat land that meets a steep, rocky, high hill called the Acrocorinth. Throughout the centuries into relatively modern times, the top of this hill has been fortified as a defensive site, and in ancient times there was probably an intention that in a time of siege the inhabitants of the city could evacuate to the top of the hill and defend themselves. As things turned out, this never happened, but the hill became a primary site for worship.

According to myth, the top of the hill belonged to Helius (another name for Apollo), the sun-god, but for some reason, Helius gave the site to Aphrodite.[1] The sanctuary of Aphrodite in the days before the city's destruction is said to have been the home of 1,000 slaves who served the goddess as sacred prostitutes. This legend gave the city an enduring reputation for licentiousness.[2] Pausanias author of a travel guide written in the 170s, about one hundred and thirty years after St. Paul's sojourn in Corinth, reported that the statue of Aphrodite on the summit was wearing armor, suggesting that she was a guardian of the city.[3] Coins issued after the reestablishment of Corinth suggest that this "guardian" was more interested in her own beauty than in protecting her people.

There was a spring at the summit of the Acrocorinth, so on a nice day people could take a walk up the mountain and be assured of refreshment when they reached the top. It would have been a nice "city park," another attraction for those who were already attracted to the temples on the mountain. Interestingly, the spring is tied to the myth of Sisyphus, the famous mythological character who was condemned to push a rock up a hill, a task which lasts for eternity because when Sisyphus nears the summit of the hill, the rock always gets away and rolls down.[4]

Was St. Paul aware of the whole myth of Sisyphus? Probably so, because it is the foundational story for the city. Most likely, in St. Paul's time no one took it seriously, but everyone knew it.

Pausanias tells us that as one traveled the path up the mountain in the year 170, one encountered ten temples, in addition to the temple of Aphrodite at the summit. These were in addition to the temples around the agora in the city. We know that not all of them had been constructed by the time of St. Paul, but some were definitely under construction during his stay. Although we don't know which ones St. Paul would have encountered, the list of Acrocorinth temples gives us a sense of the religious experience of the people.

The list Pausanias gives us seems strange, because it includes what appear to be duplicates. In fact, the "duplication" tells us something important about the ancient religions. Any god or goddess would change entirely when moved to a new location. For example, think of the complaint the Ephesian silversmiths brought against St. Paul, Acts 19:23-41. They were afraid that St. Paul's anti-idol preaching would ruin their business, so they rallied a crowd against St. Paul with the cry, "Great is Diana (or Artemis) of the Ephesians!" There were quite a few sanctuaries of Artemis in the Greek world (and Ephesus was part of the Greek world, even though it is now in modern Turkey), with names such as Artemis Alpheia, Artemis Brauronia, and Artemis Orthia,[5] but each Artemis was different from the others. The difference brought people from afar to worship in the Ephesian sanctuary and purchase Ephesian statues of Artemis. This is not to say that it was impossible to worship Artemis of Ephesus in other places. In fact, there was a statue of the Ephesian Artemis in Corinth,[6] but bowing to that statue could not replace the experience of going to Ephesus to worship in the great temple. The danger to the silversmiths was that if St. Paul was effective, no one would want to come to the great temple any more.

Similarly, the marine Isis was somehow different from the Egyptian Isis, even though we can only speculate as to what the difference was. Here is the list of temples as we proceed up the Acrocorinth:

1. Isis Pelagian, or marine.
2. Isis Egyptian.
3. Serapis Canopus (an Egyptian city).
4. Serapis without a surname.
5. Helius.
6. Necessity and Force.
7. The Mother of the gods.
8. Fates.
9. Demeter and Kore (this is the one Acrocorinth temple that has been excavated).
10. Hera Bunaea.

On the summit, a temple with images of Aphrodite, Helius, and Eros.

Notice that half of these sanctuaries are for "mystery religions" (Isis, Serapis, and Demeter). While the other temples are for traditional members of the Greek pantheon, by this time some of their worship could have taken on some of the form of mystery religions. The traditional temples might have been nothing more than monuments (such as we find in abundance in Washington, D.C.), but we know that the "mystery religion" temples were active places of worship.[7]

Each of these temples tells its own story, and we will look at a few of them in other essays, but if the basic story is, "I must go to the temple because . . .," St. Paul had two ways of countering it. First, what he reminds the Corinthians of in his first letter: because God made you, you, yourself, are God's temple (I Cor. 3:16-17). Beyond that, he may very well have talked with people in the Corinthian community about the one temple for the one God, the temple in Jerusalem (which was destroyed after the end of St. Paul's life). It certainly seems silly to have this multiplicity of temples to a multiplicity of gods. Instead of a "mount of temples," it is better to have a Temple mount.

---

1 Pausanias, p. 271.

2 See the essay, "Aphrodite and Her Girls."

3 Pausanias, p. 271.

4 For details of the myth, see the Introduction.

5 Olalla, pp. 75-83.

6 Pausanias, p. 257.

7 DeMaris.

ISIS: GODDESS OF MANY NAMES

Isis was an ancient Egyptian goddess who took over the world. In Egyptian mythology, Isis was formed as part of the early cosmos along with Osiris, Set, and several other gods and goddesses. Osiris, who began as the moon god, became prominent as the god of the underworld.[1] The ancient Egyptian documents don't tell us a lot about these three, so the story we have comes from Plutarch (died c. 125CE), who traveled to Egypt.[2] Osiris and Isis were husband and wife. Set (the personification of evil) was jealous of Osiris, and decided to kill him. At a celebration, he showed the celebrants a box, asking who would fit inside it. When Osiris lay down in the box, which had been made to fit him, Set nailed a lid on and threw it into the Nile, where it floated into the Mediterranean Sea. It finally was enclosed in a great tree which was cut down to be used as a pillar. Isis went looking for her husband, found the box in the pillar, and prepared to give him a proper burial. Set discovered the body, cut it into pieces, and scattered it. Isis once again went looking for her husband, found all but one part, and established shrines at the site of each piece. Osiris came back to life, apprehended Set, and turned him over to Isis, who then managed to let him go.

There are many details left out of this summary, and the story is a bit of a "soap opera," but in the end, Osiris reigned in the underworld with his queen, Isis. This makes a nice "happily ever after" ending, but it is not the end.

In the myth, Osiris is a "good guy." In earlier times he ruled Egypt with justice, and every Pharaoh assumed the identity of the just and capable Osiris, but Osiris is not a very "dynamic" character. Isis is dynamic. She is ambitious. She is assertive. She became the one to rule the world.

Consider this example of her assertiveness: Once upon a time, the Egyptian sun-god, Ra, was sick with some kind of infection. In spite of the fact that he was a very powerful god, he could not make himself well. Isis asked what attempts he had made to get rid of the infection. He named all of the gods whose names he had invoked in an attempt to get well, and the list did not include his own name. Names were powerful, and no god would reveal his "real" name, but Isis asked him to tell her his "real" name, so that she could use it to banish the infection. This was an amazing request, and at first Ra refused, but he finally relented, told Isis his real name, and Isis cured him.[3] From that time on, if she ever wanted to use it, she had the key to Ra's power. This is amazing arrogance on the part of Isis, and it tells us something about her personality.

About three hundred years before Christ, she showed up in Greece with a new wardrobe and a new husband, Serapis. She was apparently still queen of the underworld, and this makes us want to ask about her old husband, Osiris. Some authors claim that "Serapis" is simply an alternative name for "Osiris," but from every perspective he seems like a different fellow.

As Isis traveled around the Mediterranean world in those centuries before Christ, she took over names and titles as if they were shells on the seashore. When she appeared to Lucius in the ancient novel, *The Golden Ass*, (100 years after St. Paul) she introduced herself by a long list of names: "I, the natural mother of all life . . . the queen of those in hell . . . whose single godhead is venerated all over the earth under manifold forms, varying rites, and changing names. . . . Cecropian Minerva . . . Paphian Venus . . .Diana Dictynna . . . Stygian Prosperine . . ." etc.[4] At about the same time as *The Golden Ass*, a list of titles of Isis was prepared in Egypt. As Frederick Grant presents it to us, it takes up two full pages of closely packed text.[5]

In particular, about 1,000 years before Christ, Egyptian goddess Isis (goddess of the dead) became identified with Egyptian goddess Hathor[6] (goddess of beauty[7]). Several hundred years later in Greece she then became identified both with Demeter (goddess of spring and fertility) and Aphrodite (goddess of love and beauty). These identifications are surprising to those accustomed to thinking in categories. It would make more sense for Aphrodite and Hathor to be linked, and for Isis and Demeter to be linked, but Isis took all of them over. By the time of St. Paul, Isis was worshipped everywhere in the Roman Empire, and was a strong force in the religious life and consciousness of Corinth. This is testified by a couple of obviously personal Isis tokens (as opposed to public monuments) that have been found among the rubble of the ancient city.[8]

So, what was Isis religion about? In spite of her many names and responsibilities, she remained queen of the dead, and her religion had primarily to do with having a good life after death. In Egyptian religion, that was possible only if the deceased had been perfectly good on earth,[9] but by the time Isis moved to Europe, rituals and ceremonies had been developed to purify those belonging to the faith. At Eleisis, between Corinth and Athens, the annual purification ceremony involved driving a pig to the sea and bathing with the pig.[10]

The drawback to this approach to sanctification was cost. There were several levels of initiation, each of which had

A European priestess of Isis in uniform. They could be recognized by the knot in their robe at the center of their chest, by the milk pail in their left hand, and by the sistrum in their right hand. (Source, Erman, p. 249.) See Sistrum, p. 65.

a price. In *The Golden Ass*, the protagonist finally runs out of money, after he has passed through the initiations in Cenchreae and then, when he moved to Rome, is required to go through the initiation process all over again. Jane Harrison says that pigs were the least expensive sacrificial animal available and suggests that this means the purification ritual was available to everyone, but we can question this. After all, in the Jerusalem temple, the poor could satisfy the sacrificial requirements with inexpensive birds.

Were sexual rites involved in Isis worship at Corinth? This seems to be an open question which can be answered only after there has been excavation of the two Isis sanctuaries on the Acrocorinth. The Roman satirist, Juvenal, claimed that the only reason women went to the sanctuary was to find a sexual partner,[11] but Heyob claims that Juvenal and his friends misunderstood the cult: "It is not difficult to understand why the ancient authors and ancient society in general viewed the happenings at the Isis temple, particularly in Rome, with a great deal of suspicion. . . . because a sense of mystery surrounded the cult, the imaginations of those who were not initiates or adherents had room to conjecture about the activities at the temple. One can imagine the suspicions aroused by the practice of incubation whereby the adherent would hire a room in the temple spending the night there awaiting the appearance of one of the Egyptian gods in his dreams."[12] However, there is reason to suspect that sexual activity was part of the ritual, even if it was not a regular activity open to all initiates. At Eleusis, there was a "bridal chamber" in the sanctuary of Demeter in which ritual sexual intercourse took place.[13] Was there such a facility in the sanctuaries of Isis at Corinth? Perhaps someday we will know.

St. Paul no doubt had been acquainted with the Isis cult
from his youth, because it was in his home town of Tarsus that
Cleopatra, the Egyptian, (dressed as Isis) first met Mark Antony.[14] This meeting would still have been talked about
throughout St. Paul's boyhood, and the Isis temple in Tarsus
would have particularly remembered Cleopatra. Apart from Isis
and Osiris, most of the Egyptian gods were seen as part human,
part beast, a fact that probably relates to Romans 1:23 (And
Romans was written in Corinth). St. Paul says that "those who
suppress the truth" have "exchanged the glory of the immortal
God for images resembling a mortal human being or birds or
four-footed animals or reptiles." (Rom 1:23.) In saying this, he
echoes Octavian (Augustus) who, when fighting against Cleopatra, said, "The Egyptians worship reptiles and animals as
gods, and bestow upon their own bodies by embalmment the
glory of immortality."[15] We can be certain that, while in Corinth, St. Paul taught explicitly against the Isis cult.

---

1 Budge, p. 216.

2 Grant, pp 80-88.

3 Budge, p. 207.

4 Apuleius, p. 237.

5 Grant, pp. 128-130.

6 Merced-Ownbey, p. 7.

7 Budge, p. 156.

8 Smith.

9 Budge, pp. 228ff.

10 Harrison, pp. 152-154.

11 Juvenal (1963), p. 110, VI.487-490; and p. 151, IX.21-24 (compare 1802 edition, p. 212, VI.725-729;and pp. 308-309, IX.30-35. The verse numbering is quite different in the two editions.)

12 Heyob, pp. 112-3.

13 Harrison, p. 550.

14 Witt, p. 257, see Plutarch, "Antony," p. 352, where the reference is to the territory of Cilicia.

15 Witt, p. 255.

A priestess of Isis could have used this statue by placing a sculpture of her own head on the body. Such "ready-made" statues were common.

DᴇATH TAKᴇS NO HOLIᴅAY

Egyptian Isis was queen of the underworld. Greek Kore was queen of the underworld. Aphrodite, never one to be outdone, got involved in the underworld. (Some say that Aphrodite encouraged Kore to eat the pomegranate seeds, sealing her residence in the underworld.) Thus, the three most popular deities in Corinth were very concerned about death. The only god who wasn't concerned about death was Asclepius, the god of healing. People came to his temple with very serious medical problems (as we can see from the tokens they left behind[1]), but in his temple no one was born, no one died.

The "story" of Corinth (see the introduction for what we mean by the word "story") was a story of tragedy and death: The source of water, necessary for life, was associated with death; the great temple of Apollo, obvious to everyone in the city, was associated with death; the mythical founding king,

Sisyphus, was eternally tormented in death. It was said by some that the citizens of Corinth themselves had been either participant or complicit in the death of the children of Jason and Medea. And so it goes. Is there or has there ever been a society that tells such a sad story about itself?

It is easy to say that these ancient founding stories about Corinth were irrelevant to the citizens of St. Paul's time, but we really can't be sure about that. Consider the United States of America (a nation that tells positive and optimistic stories about itself), which is a nation of immigrants. Whenever new people come to the U.S.A., they are taught the founding stories, so that these old stories become their stories. Couldn't the same have been true in ancient Corinth? Wouldn't it have been likely that everyone in Corinth knew the stories of Peirene and the satyr who was defeated by Apollo, and Sisyphus, and the children of Medea?

The issue then is further complicated *because* of the immigrants. When Julius Caesar re-founded the city, he populated it with people of various religious backgrounds from various places. Scholars still debate exactly who was moved to the new Corinth, but it is certain that they came from various places in the Roman Empire, and brought with them customs and attitudes toward death that waged competition with one another in the amalgamated society. For centuries the Greeks had buried the dead in individual graves where they were to rest for eternity. Some of the new people believed that the most appropriate burial should be in family sepulchers: bury the individuals until their bones are clean, and then place the bones in a box along with the bones of their relatives. Others of the new people believed that cremation was the best way to care for the deceased.[2] No doubt there were other death customs that we don't know about.

Those among the population who were concerned about religion had to wonder which of these customs would best please the gods and assure a good life in the underworld. Perhaps the issue would not have been so vexing in a society with a "happy story," but in Corinth the issue was at the forefront of religious issues. In some societies the primary religious issue has to do with the nature of morality and ethics, but in Corinth the primary religious issue seems to have been with the nature of death.

Consequently, St. Paul addressed the issue: "Listen, I will tell you a mystery! We will not all die, but we will all be changed, in a moment, in the twinkling of an eye, at the last trumpet." This, St. Paul says, is the "good news" of Jesus Christ (I Cor. 15:1), and unlike the "good news" taught by the "mystery religions" of Demeter and Kore, Isis, and Dionysus, you don't have to pay a big initiation fee to learn it . . . and the "mystery" is not even a secret. Not only do you sign no oath of secrecy, you are even encouraged to tell others about the "mystery."

Growing from this "mystery" is a religious rite that may have been unique to the Corinthian congregation, baptism for the dead, which St. Paul mentions briefly (I Cor 15:29) after having already warned them not to place too much confidence in baptism (I Cor 10:1-13). The classic commentary by Robertson and Plummer says the meaning of the phrase, "baptism for the dead" is "doubtful," citing an 1890 article in which the author, J. W. Horsley, collected thirty-six explanations. Of the various explanations, today most commentators presume that the Corinthians were practicing vicarious baptism for individuals who had died. Tertullian (150 years after St. Paul) agrees that this is what they were doing. Tertullian then says, "His only aim in alluding to it was that he might all the more firmly insist upon the resurrection of the body, in proportion as they who were vainly baptized for the dead resorted to the practice from their belief of such a resurrection."[3] In other words, by Tertullian's time the practice was unheard of other than the one reference in First Corinthians, and Tertullian didn't like it. However, in a death-saturated society such as Corinth seemed to be, idiosyncratic measures such as vicarious baptism for those who have already died are to be expected. Repeating what Tertullian said: St. Paul didn't say that he approved of the practice, he simply used the reference to it to make his logical argument.

What, then, about cremation? The issue is as vital today as it was 2,000 years ago. If resurrection is reviving a corpse, then there is no hope if there is no corpse. This was the belief of the ancient Egyptians, and Robertson and Plummer[4] quote an anonymous Jewish document written half a century after St. Paul as affirming the need for a corpse, because the resurrection body will be no different from the earthly body:

> In what shape will those live who live in Thy day?
> Will they then resume this form of the present,
> and put on these entrammeling members?
> And He answered and said to me: The earth
> will assuredly restore the dead, which it now
> receives in order to preserve them, making
> no change in their form, but as it has received,
> so will it restore them. (*Apocalypse of Baruch*,
>   xlix. 2, 3, l. 1, 2.)

Such a doctrine of resuscitation leaves no hope for many people whose bodies have been utterly torn apart into their constituent molecules, and St. Paul argues that a resuscitated body would be incapable of eternal life. So he goes through a long argument that is characteristic of Greek philosophy.

Robertson and Plummer summarize the conclusion thus:

> vv. 50-57. The two objections are now answered.
> How is resurrection possible after the body has
> been dissolved in the grave? Answer: the difficulty
> is the other way: resurrection would be impossible
> without such dissolution, for it is dissolution that
> frees the principle of new life. Then what kind of a
> body do the risen have, if the present body is not
> restored? Answer: a body similar to that of the
> risen Lord, *i.e.*, a body as suitable to the condition
> of the new life as a material body is to the present
> physical condition.
>
> But a further question may be raised. What
> will happen to those believers who are alive when
> the Lord comes? The radical translation from
> *psuchikon* to *pneumatikon* must take place,
> whether through death or not. Mortal must become
> immortal. God will make the victory over death in
> all cases complete.

So it was an important issue in St. Paul's time, but why is it important today? Why would a resurrection body be important, other than the idea giving emotional solace to those in grief? Here is a personal answer on the part of the author:

When we think of the "body" in the abstract, not as our present body with arms and legs, lungs and intestines, blood and bones, but as some unimaginable, undefined "body," we can ask about this abstract body, "What purpose does it serve?" I suggest our body serves at least three purposes, and the resurrection body, whatever it "looks like" or how it is constructed, would have to serve the same purposes:

1. It puts us in a location, so that we don't spread all over the place, like fog.
2. It gives us a spatial orientation so we know up from down, right from left.
3. It individualizes us, so we can recognize each other.

---

[1] See essay, "The Ancient Hospital," p. 104.

[2] DeMaris, 1995-A and 1995-B, p. 113.

[3] Tertullian, *Adversus Marcion*, Bk. 5, Ch. 10.

[4] Robertson and Plummer, p. 368, fn.

KOR€'S €AST€R

Let's go north from Corinth to the city of Athens, and back in time, about 450 years before St. Paul's visit, and attend the theatre. We could see a new play by the comedy writer, Aristophanes, called *The Thesmophoriazusae*. This tongue-twisting title has been discarded by several translators in exchange for more attractive titles. For example, one old English title is "Euripides and the Women of Athens." This is not a bad title, because the play pokes fun at the ancient Greek playwright, Euripides (a contemporary of Aristophanes) and his apparent antipathy toward women (and tells how the women got even with him). However, the "tongue-twisting" title is useful for us, because it refers directly to one of the festivals of the goddesses Demeter and Kore, called "Thesmophoria," celebrated in Athens in mid-October.[1]

This festival was celebrated over a four day period, and no men were allowed to participate or to view the ritual. Of course, we might reasonably ask how Aristophanes knew enough about the festival to write the play, which involves a man caught spying on the festival, but we simply have to take the play (with a grain of salt, remembering above all that it's a comedy) for whatever it might be worth. (We have the same problem with other fictional descriptions of the "mystery religions," such as the *Bacchae* by Euripides, which is about female worship of Dionysus, as well as the fictional description of Isis worship in *The Golden Ass* of Apulieus.) As one scholar says, what we know about worship in the mystery religions "must be reconstructed from a multitude of sources whose reliability is uneven, yielding a composite image which is at best an approximation."[2]

In spite of these historical difficulties and cautions, it will be interesting for us to look at the celebration, day by day.

The first day was a day of preparation. The women went to the temple and made ready to stay there during the days of celebration.

The second day was a memorial of the descent of Persephone (also known as Kore) into Hades. We know nothing about the ritual celebration on this day, but we have evidence that the rituals of the mystery religions involved reenactment of the stories related to the religions. If so, the day might begin with dancing, a memory of the story that Kore was abducted by Hades while she was in a meadow picking flowers. Then, as the ritual proceeded, Kore would leave the scene, disappearing into the underworld, and the day that began in joy would end in gloom. Perhaps there was a propitiatory sacrifice at the end of the day.

The third day was a day of bereavement. According to the myth, after Kore had been abducted by Hades, her mother Demeter searched everywhere for her, carrying a torch in her hand. It seems likely that the women in the temple would use flaming torches. The women would fast, and act out a mourning ritual.

The fourth, and final day of the celebration, would memorialize Kore coming back to earth. The myth tells us that Demeter was able to work out a compromise with Hades whereby Kore would spend half the year with her underworld husband (autumn and winter on earth) and half the year above ground with her mother (spring and summer on earth).

What does this much older Athenian festival have to do with the worship of Demeter and Kore in the Corinth of St. Paul's time? One parallel is certain: the worship of Demeter and Kore in Corinth was a secret belonging to women. Pausanius tells us that casual visitors weren't even allowed to see the statues in the temple. This much suggests that the rituals might also have survived over 450 years. Our own experience confirms this possibility: the living religions of our time have had stable rituals over a period of hundreds and thousands of years.

So, was this an "Easter" celebration? Did St. Paul teach his congregation something different about Easter? Nothing helps us clarify our own thinking better than an intellectual challenge. At first glance, it appears that there is a similarity between Easter and Thesmophoria. Christians begin their celebration with 40 days of general spiritual preparation, and then on Good Friday most congregations set up the worship area in a little different way than normal. Thursday evening is often a memorial of the footwashing and/or the Last Supper. At noon on Good Friday, it is common for the faithful to gather for a memorial of the crucifixion, following a ritual that is an intellectual reenactment: the seven last words. Alternatively or in addition, the faithful may gather on Friday evening for an intellectual reenactment called Tenebrae, or the service of darkness. Thursday evening and Good Friday could be compared to the second day of *Thesmophoria*. There is also a similarity between *Thesmophoria* and Holy Saturday. And then we have Easter.

There are many popular books and lecturers who claim that primitive Christianity was no different from any of the "mystery religions," but, contrary to what the contemporary lecturers would have us believe, this claim is not new, and it has been shown to be invalid. For example, John Franklin Troupe clearly expressed the differences in 1917,[3] and Bruce Metzger spoke to the issue in 1955.[4]

Let's briefly think about Easter, the celebration of the resurrection of Jesus. Is this the same as Kore coming back from her home in the underworld? Kore's home and husband were in the underworld. She only came back to earth to visit. Her devotees were happy to have her visit, just as we might be happy to have our adult children come back for a visit, but these adult children have established a home elsewhere. Furthermore, Kore's devotees expect her to return to earth on a regular schedule. Jesus rose only once.

There is much more that could be said, but let's move back to Holy Saturday. When Kore was underground with her husband, the mythology gives us no sense that she was, at that time, concerned about anyone else, living or dead. In contrast,

Schematic of a typical resurrection icon. Christ, standing on the broken doors of Hell is pulling Adam and Eve out of their coffins.

for millennia Christians have affirmed what is commonly known as the "Apostles' Creed," in which with reference to Saturday, they say, "He descended into hell." The understanding behind this simple phrase is that in spite of his crucifixion, Jesus maintained a concern for people, and went to the realm of the dead for their salvation. In Eastern Orthodox Christianity, there is an iconic motif displayed in a vast number of church buildings which shows Christ standing on the broken-down gates of hell, pulling up one or two people by the wrist. In some pictures one person is being pulled up, and it is Adam. In other pictures, both Adam and Eve are being pulled up. In either case, the icon is a graphic portrayal of Christ's concern for all people (in contrast with Kore's lack of concern for any people).

And there is Good Friday. Metzger says it well: "In all the Mysteries which tell of a dying deity, the god dies by compulsion and not by choice, sometimes in bitterness and despair, never in a self-giving love."[5] Kore's disappearance was a result of the lust of Hades. In contrast, Jesus submitted to arrest, "trial" and crucifixion.

Clearly, the narratives are different. The *Thesmophoria* is not Easter.

---

[1] B. B. Rogers, an editor of the text, comments, "Of course we are considering the Athenian *Thesmophoria* only. At other places, the *Thesmophoria* were celebrated at different times, and in a different manner." Aristophenes (tr. Rogers) 1904. p. vii, note 4.

[2] Kraemer, p. 56.

[3] Troupe.

[4] Metzger.

[5] Metzger, p. 17.

THE MAIDEN GETS MEAN

The basic story of Demeter is simple: Demeter, the goddess of spring fertility had a daughter. The god of the underworld lusted after the daughter, found her alone one day, and forcibly took her to the underworld to be his queen. When Demeter discovered that her daughter was gone, she went into such deep mourning that she couldn't do her appointed task of bringing the season of spring to earth. Intercessions were made, a compromise was reached, and the daughter was permitted to return during spring and summer to be with her mother. In the fall, she returned to her husband in the underworld, and the earth, in mourning, saw vegetation die and cold weather return.

In Greek, the daughter's name was Persephone, and the Romans called her Prosperina, but the Corinthians simply called her Kore, the Maiden, whom we tend to assume was the virginal innocent child who was kidnapped by the mean god, Hades, with help from the unreliable god, Hermes. Kore's press agents want us to feel sorry for her.

Maybe there is nothing to feel sorry about. Kore could have come back to her mother if she had not eaten while in the underworld. As it happens, she had snacked on some pomegranate seeds. We should be suspicious. How hungry was she, really? She didn't eat a meal, just a snack. Did she know nothing about the rules? Let's remember that she was an adolescent, full of raging hormones and a desire to get away from the restrictions of home life. Maybe she wanted to be "kidnapped."

If you're ready to say that this interpretation is "blaming the victim," hold off for a little bit.

On the slopes of the Acrocorinth, there was a temple to Demeter (one of ten temples on the trail up to the summit of the mountain), and at this point, it is the only temple on the slopes to have been excavated.[1] The temple had been constructed about 500 years before the birth of Jesus, fell into disrepair after the destruction of Corinth (although the cult of Demeter did not die out), and was rebuilt and remodeled before and during the time that St. Paul was in the city. (Major construction projects took a long time.)

The excavation of this temple has shown us some interesting things. First, the cult was primarily a women's cult. Second, it changed its theological focus when the government changed from Greek to Roman.[2] Prior to the destruction of Corinth, the temple had emphasized the worship of Demeter as goddess of agriculture. After the reestablishment of Corinth, the worship centered on Kore, queen of the underworld. A hundred or more years after St. Paul, someone named Octavios Agathopous donated a floor mosaic to the temple that pictures two baskets with two large snakes wrapped around them. The basket is an old Demeter/Kore symbol, and the snake is often a symbol of the underworld. The dedication of the mosaic seems to be to Kore, not to Demeter. In addition, a number of pottery fragments have been found at the temple picturing baskets in conjunction with snakes.

Now we can think back to the question of whether Kore might not have wanted to be queen of the underworld, and not have objected to her "abduction" by Hades. By being queen of the underworld, she gained quite a bit of prestige.

Not only did she gain prestige by being queen of the underworld, it appears that she was also in a good position to offer advice to other young women who wanted to get married. The evidence we have for this comes, not from Corinth, but from Locri, and not from the time of St. Paul, but from several hundred years earlier, but it seems worth thinking about.[3] At Locri archeologists found a series of clay relief plaques in the sanctuary of Persephone. In these plaques we see various gods and mortals honoring Persephone (that is, Kore) as a bride and giving her gifts appropriate for a bride, including cocks.

Let's think about the cock. "The cock appears to have been very closely connected with Persephone at Locri. . . . [apparently] the cock was sacred to Persephone . . . in the Greek world in general. [For Greeks] the cock had two main symbolic connotations. Firstly, maleness, in the double sense of bravery and fighting spirit, and of male sexuality; and secondly, the terrifying things of this world and especially death. . . . The cock in a specifically nuptial context can be seen as symbolizing maleness, including male sexuality and aggressiveness, harnessed into marriage . . ."[4] In other words, young girls with raging hormones came to worship a goddess whose raging hormones had helped her attain a position of high prestige, so that they might control the male of their choice, just as Kore had finally controlled the male Hades.

In St. Paul's time, young women who wanted to get married came to the temple of the queen of the underworld. We know this because of some startling requests left at the temple. In the time of St. Paul and after, it was apparently common for young women to leave requests for Kore to do bad things to their romantic rivals. The archeologists found rolled up sheets of lead in the temple, and when they unrolled them, they were found to be inscribed with curse prayers, almost all of them calling for curses on women.

Perhaps we should pity a girl named Karpile Babbia. Three of the curse prayers are directed against her: "I consign and entrust Karpile Babbia, the weaver of garlands, to the Fates who extract justice, so that they may expose her acts of insolence . . . so that they may overcome and completely destroy her and her heart and her mind and the wits of Karpile Babbia."[5] Apparently such curses were common across the ancient world,[6] but no matter how much of a witch or vamp Karpile Babbia may have been, the curse against her leaves us with shivers. The issue is clearly love rivalry, as one of the curse–prayers includes the petition, "make me fertile."[7]

Clearly Kore, the innocent maiden, could be really mean! Could Christ be equally mean? If you lived in Corinth and were part of the congregation started by St. Paul, you might think so. As an ancient Corinthian looked around it seemed that the rules of religion were clear: make an alliance with a particular god, honor that god properly, and then ask the god for what you want, even (or especially) the destruction of your enemies.

This brings us to I Cor. 12:3, one of the most puzzling texts in the New Testament: "Wherefore I give you to understand, that no man speaking by the Spirit of God calleth Jesus accursed: and [that] no man can say that Jesus is the Lord, but by the Holy Ghost." (KJV) Perhaps returning to the Authorized or King James Version emphasizes the shock value of this verse. What is St. Paul talking about? Who in the world, as a follower of Jesus, would call Jesus accursed?

Bruce Winter suggests that the curse-prayers to Kore help us understand I Cor. 12:3. Translators have uniformly translated the first part of the verse as something like "Jesus is cursed," because in the Greek text of the New Testament, the second part of the verse is grammatically parallel: "Jesus is Lord." Grammar, however, is tricky, and Winter says that it now seems clear that St. Paul was cautioning the followers of Jesus against assuming that Jesus is simply a pagan god.[8] Paul is really saying that no one, speaking by the Spirit of God, can call on Jesus to curse anyone.

We know that the Corinthian congregation was severely divided. Perhaps there were even prayers being offered that Jesus would "overcome and completely destroy" certain other members of the congregation.

Even today we sometimes get really upset with others in our congregation, and we, also, might want to pray that Jesus might curse them, but then we remember the stories of Jesus in the Gospels. There are lots of applicable ones, but Winter suggests, in particular, Luke 9:54-55. When the disciples wanted to curse a village with destruction, Jesus forbade it.[9]

1 Bookidis and Stroud.

2 DeMaris.

3 Sourvinou-Inwood.

4 Sourvinou-Inwood, p. 108.

5 Bookidis and Stroud, p. 30.

6 Winter.

7 Winter, p. 168.

8 Winter, p. 178.

9 Winter, p. 179.

DIONYSUS AS A CORINTHIAN

Classical scholars have generally accepted the notion that ancient Greek religious rituals were largely reenactments of the stories in mythology. As Noel Robertson says, "A myth was told to explain a rite, and at the end of the telling the rite was held up as proof that the myth had happened so."[1] He goes on to give an example: It is said that the adolescent Dionysus went mad, then he met his mother on a mountain and she cured him by sitting him on a throne and having Corybantes dance around him. Thus, the mystery cult involved placing an initiate or a mental patient on a throne and dancing wildly around that person."[2]

In contrast, Harvard professor Albert Henrichs makes a good argument that there was a difference between the way the god was worshipped in rural areas and in urban areas. He also argues that we should not assume that the myths associated with the god accurately represent the views of the worshipping cult. In his words, the "Roman Dionysus was benign, pastoral and peaceful, a recipient of cult and a divine example of a relaxed lifestyle who offered physical and mental escape from the burdens of the day and the ills of progressive urbanization."[3] In other words, the Dionysus of Roman Athens was simply a god of hedonism—his temple was a nice club in which to get drunk.[4]

Likewise, Robert Turcan says that in the Roman Empire, "costumed banquets replaced the drunkenness of the Maenads who roamed far from the towns, among the pine trees and rocks."[5] How important was the story of a god? Did mythology really have anything to do with religious sentiment and worship? It seems that both Robertson and Heinrichs are correct in their way, and this little debate tells us something about what St. Paul would have found when he visited Corinth.

In Italy, 186 BCE (40 years before the destruction of Corinth), there had been a great scandal related to the great annual celebration of Dionysus: a particular important person was invited to become an initiate, but the invitation was a cover for an assassination plot. In the secrecy of the cult celebration, the "initiate" was going to be poisoned. The plot was discovered, and the Roman government outlawed the cult. Later, when the Roman Empire was established, the government saw use in the cult of Dionysus. Mark Antony once entered Ephesus "behind a procession of Bacchantes, Pans and Satyrs, to the sound of the Pan-pipes and flutes: he was acclaimed as a New Dionysus."[6] The cult was again legal, but it was carefully monitored throughout the Empire and initiations were more symbolic, although they ended in drunkenness.[7] Since the reestablished Corinth was a Roman colony, the formal restrictions on the cult would have applied there as well as in Rome.

However, when it comes to getting around restrictions people are endlessly creative, and evidence from Corinth suggests that we ought to pay some attention to the myth behind the worship. Dionysus was the god of the pleasures of wine and theatre, but there were also often overtones of sexuality in his worship, and he also had a role in life after death.

According to the myths, Dionysus was a child of Zeus under a really strange set of circumstances. First, Zeus raped the beautiful Persephone (who happened to be one of his daughters) by changing himself into a snake. Consequently, she gave birth to Dionysus, but the jealous Titans killed the infant and ate him. Zeus was able to preserve the infant's heart, so he proceeded to rape Semele, impregnating her with a second Dionysus who had the heart of the first. Zeus' wife, Hera, was jealous of Semele, and plotted to get her killed.

The plot was extremely clever. Hera disguised herself and came to the pregnant Semele, advising her that she should be certain about the "man" who fathered her child. If he really was a god, he should be able to appear as a god. "Semele, you should ask him to appear to you in his fll glory. If he is a god, he can do it, and if he is not really a god, you will find out." When Semele asked to see the glory, Zeus tried to convince her that a vision of the full glory would be fatal to any human, but Semele insisted, and Zeus had earlier promised to give her any gift she asked. Zeus glorified himself, and Semele died (as Hera knew she would), but at her death she delivered the premature baby. Zeus incubated the infant "in his thigh" until he could be brought forth, nursed and raised. Because of this, he is sometimes given the title, "twice born."

This second Dionysus was raised in the wild with nymphs, satyrs, and other minor mythical creatures of the field so that the Titans wouldn't find him. He discovered how to make wine, and traveled the world teaching people about the glories of his wine. Incidentally, we are told that three times he used his wine to inebriate females so that he could have sexual relations with them.[8]

We see the idea of worship mirroring mythology in *Bacchae*, a play by Euripides. When Dionysus was raised in the wild, he must have dressed in wild skins, so his followers

Ancient Greek vase painting showing a drunken Dionysus dancing and ripping a fawn in two. (From Harrison, p. 459.)

are shown in the play and in vase paintings as wearing deer skins over their shoulders as they celebrated "out in the woods."

Drunkenness led to wild behavior climaxed by tearing apart a living wild animal and eating the raw flesh. This was possibly an enactment of the Titans tearing apart the infant Dionysus. In the play of Euripides, it is the disrespectful king who is torn apart by drunken women who are duped by the god to think the king is a wild lion.

Euripides is showing us the sort of ancient wild celebration-in-the-woods that Henrichs says was abandoned when the cult of Dionysus moved to the city. We need to look more closely at this "civilized" version of Dionysus.

Although we have statues of Dionysus from Roman Corinth, we have no reference to any Corinthian temple dedicated to the god, although some relics related to Dionysus were found in the excavation of the temple to Demeter and Kore (or Persephone), so quite possibly the Corinthian celebrations of Dionysus were held at his first mother's temple. In Corinth, Dionysus seems to have been seen by devotees as helping Demeter thresh the grain, a surprisingly domestic task for the wild god.[9] A dining room was associated with the temple, so maybe Henrichs is right and instead of a wild feast on raw meat, the Corinthian devotees had a civil meal—maybe the meat was even cooked.

What does "civilized" mean? We have been given a glimpse at such "civilized" rites by the ancient writer Lucian:

> A festival at Athens which contains mysteries of Demeter, Kore, and Dionysus upon the cutting of the vine and the tasting of the wine already in store,

taking place at Athens, in which they display things
resembling male genitals, about which they
relate that they came into being as a security
for human procreation, because Dionysus in
giving wine provided this drug as an incitement
to intercourse.[10]

A Corinthian memory of the "wild" Dionysus is at-
tested by Pausanias, the travel writer who came to Corinth
about 100 years after St. Paul. He tells us that he found
"wooden images of Dionysus, which are covered with gold
with the exception of their faces; these are ornamented with red
paint." He then explains that these two "images" were made
from the tree that the king had climbed to view the rites of Dionysus before he was attacked by the women and torn to pieces,
the event portrayed in Euripides' play.[11] In other words, even
though the religious celebrations may have been "toned down,"
the heritage of wild celebrations in the forest was not forgotten,
and neither was the "wild" god with a streak of merciless
vengeance. Dionysus was, among other things, a phallic
god,[12] and the two wooden poles in Corinth were probably testimonies to the god's phallic nature.[13]

Another testimony to the remembered heritage of the
"wild" Dionysus is a damaged and probably unfinished carving,
less than three feet tall (restored size would be at most 3 ft.)
showing a nymph "struggling to free herself from the advances
of Dionysus, whom Pan seems to be encouraging or supporting
in the struggle."[14] This carving was apparently left over from
Greek times, but still around in the time of St. Paul. It seems
that the licentious reputation of Corinth was buttressed by Dionysus as well as by Aphrodite.

Scenes from an elaborately carved sarcophagus in the British Museum. Top, a faithful drunken man, supported by friends, leads the parade into Heaven. Bottom, perhaps we see the "original" pink elephants of drunken delusion.

In addition to drunkenness and possible sexual relations, the cult of Dionysus provided assurances about life after death. Initiates were given "passwords" to get them through the perils of the underworld, and were assured that just as Dionysus had brought his mother, Semele, up from the dead, so would Dionysus save them. He could do this because he, himself, had died and come back to life many times.[15] Sarcophagi show us what members of the cult expected: Dionysus would bring them into a future life of marvelous drunken stupor.

For whatever reason, the cult of Dionysus seemed to be particularly attractive to women. This was especially true in the Greek world, but continued in the Roman world, even though more men became followers under Rome, so that some associations were exclusively male.[16] The Romans were more open to letting women "mix" with men than the Greeks, so it is not surprising to find that the cult of Dionysus frequently had men and women at the same ritual.

One feature of the rites of Dionysus was cross-dressing, a custom that endured for more than 1,000 years. In 692 CE, the Church Fathers decreed "that no man put on women's clothing nor any woman men's clothing; that they not wear comic, satiric, or tragic masks; that they not shout out the name of the execrable Dionysus while pressing the grapes or while pouring the wine into kegs."[17]

Drunkenness, licentiousness, cross-dressing, and a magical view of life after death. St. Paul had some work to do. Certainly Euripides had written *the Bacchae* several hundred years earlier, and certainly the standards of cult worship had changed, but probably the character of the god had not changed. Euripides portrayed him is immature, self-centered and vengeful. Contrast the story of the pleasure-seeking Dionysus with the story of Jesus, "who, though he was in the form of God, did not regard equality with God as something to be exploited, but emptied himself, taking the form of a slave . . . humbled himself and became obedient to the point of death." (Philippians 2:6-8.)

Of course we cannot read St. Paul's mind in order to claim that he wrote certain things to counter particular elements in Corinthian culture, but we can readily imagine the members of the Corinthian congregation (and anyone else who heard the message) thinking about Dionysus and recognizing the contrast.

"The message about the cross is foolishness to those who are perishing, but to us who are being saved it is the power of God" (I Cor 1:18). This introduces a passage on "wisdom," but it also speaks to those who sought salvation in hedonism.

"You cannot drink the cup of the Lord and the cup of demons. You cannot partake of the table of the Lord and the table of demons." (I Cor 10:21.) Every god and goddess had feasts, but for Dionysus, the cup was the cup of drunkenness, and the table was the table of savagely killed raw meat.

"Does not nature itself teach you that if a man wears long hair, it is degrading to him . . .?" (I Cor 11:14.) Youthful statues of Dionysus portrayed him with long hair, and he was the only male god with such hair.

"If, therefore, the whole church comes together and all speak in tongues, and outsiders or unbelievers enter, will they not say that you are out of your mind?" (I Cor 14:23.) The secret initiation into the cult of Dionysus apparently involved a ceremony of madness.

"Death has been swallowed up in victory!" (I Cor 15:54.) For the mystery religions: Isis, Demeter, Dionysus, there was no hope of "victory" over death. Death was the husband of Persephone (Kore), who was the mother of Dionysus. Osiris, husband of Isis, was lord of death.

"Therefore I am content with weaknesses, insults, hardships, persecutions, and clamities for the sake of Christ; for whenever I am weak, then I am strong." (II Cor 12:10.) No follower of Dionysus would say this. No Platonist would say this. No one, other than a "Cynic," would say this, unless that person was St. Paul.

---

1 Robertson, p. 220. Harrison asserts that, "The myth of the rape of Persephone of course really arose from the ritual, not the ritual from the myth." (p. 124.) No matter which way the cause and effect worked, ritual and myth went together so that rituals were reenactments of myths.

2 Robertson, p. 222.

3 Henrichs.

4 See essay "Sacramental Drunkenness.

5 Turcan, p. 297.

6 Turcan, p. 307.

7 Turcan, pp. 301-312.

8 The complicated story of Dionysus is found in scattered sources. For a history of the character, see Harrison, pp. 359-379. For the general story, see a standard book on mythology,

such as Murray, pp. 128-132, or Howe and Harper, pp. 83-85. See also Robertson, pp. 218-219. For a discussion of the story from a psychoanalytic perspective, see Newbold.

9 Ure, pp. 120-121.

10 Quoted by Csapo, p. 267.

11 Pausanius, Book II, Chapter ii, para. 6-7, LCC pp. 257-259.

12 There is a famous phallic statue dedicated to Dionysus on the Greek island of Delos.

13 Csapo, p. 284.

14 Richardson, p. 288.

15 Turcan, p. 313.

16 The association in Athens referred to in the essay "Sacramental Drunkenness" seems to have been restricted to men.

17 Quoted by Csapo, p. 263.

A couple memorialized on a Hellenistic grave marker.

SACRAMENTAL DRUNKENNESS

Consider I Cor 11:20-21. "When you come together, it is not to eat the Lord's supper. For when the time comes to eat, each of you goes ahead with your own supper, and one goes hungry and another becomes drunk."

We must ask if St. Paul is using a rhetorical exaggeration here. Is it possible that the Corinthians thought it was all right to become drunk at a service of worship to God Almighty? We find that the answer is, "Yes." Drunkenness in the Corinthian culture might indeed be an aspect of worship. And three chapters later, St. Paul saw reason to come back to this general theme: let there not be "disorder," but "peace" at worship (and presumably the worshipful meals)—I Cor. 14:33, and see that everything happens "decently and in order"—I Cor. 14:40. To a degree, St. Paul was simply instructing congregation members to observe common sense courtesy.[1] Robertson and Plummer's classic commentary points out that

Socrates instructed students not to get drunk unless there was enough wine for everyone to get drunk together.[2] Is courtesy our only concern when the faithful gather? Is courtesy the extent of the Gospel?

The god Dionysus, also known as Bacchus, was an important deity in Corinthian culture. Consider the famous floor mosaic that was found in the house of a rich Corinthian. No one spends the money on an expensive mosaic floor to celebrate an insignificant god.

Young Dionysus in floor mosaic.

Dionysus had a legitimate place in the traditional pantheon of Greek gods. He was a son of the great god, Zeus, but he couldn't be held in check by the pantheon.[3] By the time of St. Paul, the worship of Dionysus had grown to be independent of the ancient worship of Zeus and the rest of the pantheon. The cult of Dionysus had become one of the many flourishing "mystery religions."

The god responsible for discovering the ingredients and process for making wine was seen, in his "mystery religion" incarnation as having delivered the secret of eternal life. The playwright, Euripides, writing four centuries prior to St. Paul, had one of his characters speak in praise of "this new god," Dionysus, saying that the two greatest gods are Demeter (fertility of the soil) and Dionysus, whose gift of wine "gives rest from grief to men . . . there is none other balm for toils [than drunken forgetfulness]." Earthly drunken forgetfulness was also seen as the basic blessing of heaven, where the faithful can spend eternity in a drunken stupor. Not everyone accepted this doctrine of drunkenness and within the mystery religions there was a theological debate (leading to denominational splits) as to whether spirits in the land of the dead drank from the well of forgetfulness or from the well of memory.[4]

A wealthy member of the "denomination" of drinking-too-much commissioned an elaborately carved sarcophagus which is now on display in the British Museum. The carving is evidently a procession leading the faithful into "heaven." (See p. 155.) At the head of the procession, the clearly drunken celebrant is being supported by a friend, and at the rear are two elephants (would they be the "pink elephants" of bar-room fame?) ridden by two "eros" figures. In between, all sorts of people and creatures are dancing and celebrating. If this is "heaven," would it be reflected in earthly worship? Does the sarcophagus in some sense represent liturgy in the cult of Dionysus? Is this scene not only a parade into "heaven," but also a portrayal of a sacrament of drunkenness?

We also have a fascinating document from a Dionysus society in Attica (Athens). It is not from Corinth, and it is dated about 120 years after St. Paul's time in Greece, but let's assume that it describes the basic character of any Dionysus society, including the Dionysus society in St. Paul's Corinth.   It is a set of club by-laws that is, in form, similar to the by-laws of any organization we might belong to today. In these by-laws, among other things we read the following:[5]

✧   No one may either sing or create a disturbance or applaud at the gatherings, but each shall say and act his allotted part with all good order and quietness under the direction of the priest.

✧   If anyone start a fight or be found acting disorderly or occupying the seat of any other member or using insulting or abusive language to anyone, the person so abused or insulted shall produce two of the Iobacchi to state upon oath that they heard him insulted or abused, and he who was guilty of the insult or abuse shall pay to the Society twenty-five light drachmas.

✧   If anyone come to blows, he who has been struck shall lodge a written statement with the priest or the vice-priest, and he shall without fail convene a general meeting, and the Iobacchi shall decide the question by vote under the presidency of the priest, and the penalty shall be exclusion for a period to be determined and a fine not exceeding twenty-five silver denarii.
          And no one shall deliver a speech without the leave of the priest or the vice priest on pain of being liable to a fine of thirty light drachmas to the Society.

✧   The orderly officer shall be chosen by lot or appointed by the priest, and he shall bear the thyrsus of the god to him who is disorderly or creates a disturbance. And anyone beside whom the thyrsus is laid shall, with the approval of the priest or of the arch-bacchus, leave the banqueting hall; but if he disobey, the "horses" who shall be appointed by the priests shall take him up and put him outside the front door and he shall be liable to the punishment inflicted upon those who fight.[6]

What is all of this about? Clearly the rules we have quoted are intended to keep some sort of order at a drunken celebration. No drunken singing or other noise making, no fighting, no making of drunken speeches, and if you do these things there is a clear method of discipline and a clear system of punitive fines. This drunken organization also has it bouncers, the "horses."

Back to St. Paul's letter. Did Corinthian Christians get drunk at the Lord's supper? Probably so, because they had the model before them of the worship of Dionysus.

At the initiation into the cult of Dionysus, the members apparently watched and participated in dramatizations and group enactments of the myths surrounding Dionysus. (Some of them were possibly sexual, with the whole group getting involved, but that doesn't concern us at this point.) In other words, the members learned the basic stories of the cult.

With what stories would a Christian preacher or teacher counter the stories of Dionysus? Let's try this:

"Hear, my child, and be wise, and direct your mind in the way. Do not be among the winebibbers, or among the gluttonous eaters of meat; For the drunkard and the glutton will come to poverty, and drowsiness will clothe them with rags." (Proverbs 23:19-21.)

"Go the ant, your lazybones; consider its ways and be wise. Without having any chief or officer or ruler, it prepares its food in summer and gathers its sustenance in harvest. How long will you lie there, O lazybones? When will you rise from your sleep? A little sleep, a little slumber, a little folding of the hands to rest, and poverty will come upon you like a robber, and want like an armed warrior." (Proverbs 6:6-11.)

---

1 See the essay on "Common Meals."

2 Robertson and Plummer, p. 241.

3 For background on the myth of Dionysus, see the essay, "Dionysus as a Corinthian."

4 Harrison, pp. 576-581. See also pp. 446ff, where she asserts that classical Greeks seldom drank too much. A careful reading reveals that "too much" is intentionally undefined, and it may be that Harrison and St. Paul would have disagreed. See her essay against Puritanism, pp. 452-453.

5 Ferguson, Everett. *Backgrounds of Early Christianity*, second edition. William B. Eerdmans, 1993, pp. 134-135.

6 The "thyrsus," was the staff of Dionysus, consisting of a rod with a pine cone at the top and/or with a grape vine around it. Murray, p. 132; Euripides, *Bacchae* 25 (p. 350) translated as "ivied javelin." See also illuatration in Harrison, p. 398, reproduced here:

WATER, MYSTERY AND MAGIC

One reason the isthmus was an excellent site for a city is its ample water supply. Although Corinth receives less rainfall than other sites in Greece, the site has a geological structure that stores and provides a great deal of easily accessible water. Landon has identified twenty-four individual springs within the ancient city walls![1] In the "downtown" area (called the agora by the Greeks, and the forum by the Romans) there were three famous springs, the Perine (possibly the most famous ancient water source anywhere), the Glauce (or Glauke), and located between them, the "Sacred Spring."

The Sacred Spring was not a source of water for daily use, but was exclusively a site for some sort of worship, probably a form of "mystery religion" with a special concern about death. The temple associated with the Sacred Spring seems to have gone out of use after the destruction of Corinth in 146 BCE, and by the time of St. Paul's sojourn in Corinth, the Sacred Spring had been covered by the "northwest shops," one of the sites where St. Paul might have had his tent-making business.

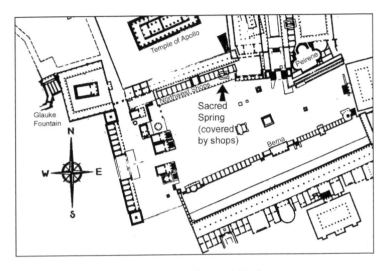

Location of the Sacred Spring

We might think that the cult of the Sacred Spring would be irrelevant to our interest in Corinthian culture at the time when St. Paul was there, but one feature of the old Sacred Spring temple attracts our attention and fires our imagination. The temple was a fairly small space, with an altar in the midst of the room. Apparently, at some point during the ritual, a priest would pour water over the altar. The water would then run through a long channel to a wall, and would then pour into a container located on the far side of the wall. Apparently most of the celebrants would gather on the far side of the wall, where the container captured the water. (They might have been engaged in some cultic activity outside the wall, such as a torch race.)

Right next to the water-channel was a tunnel, large enough for an adult to crawl through on hands and knees. Both the channel and the tunnel were covered by a stone roof, and it was possible for a man or woman in the tunnel to reach a hand into the water-channel. The access to the tunnel was through a secret entrance near the wall, and there was a sign outside the tunnel area warning unauthorized people to stay away. The tunnel ended inside the temple with a "megaphone-shaped" opening.

Two speculations have been made about this tunnel and water-channel. (1) A man or woman in the tunnel could speak as the voice of a god or goddess in answer to questions from the faithful who were inside the temple. (2) Someone inside the tunnel could carry a small dam and a full wineskin. At the appropriate time, they could stop the flow of water with the dam, and pour wine into the channel. Only a small group could fit into the temple, and probably a larger group would be gathered outside the wall. This larger group would witness the changing of water into wine.[2]

This is simply speculation. We don't even know what god or goddess was worshipped in this temple, although the current best guess is that it was Kotyto, a somewhat obscure heroine. The various ambiguous stories about her contradict one another, and it is difficult to understand exactly why she was worshipped and what form the worship might have taken.[3] Since the Sacred Spring worship did not endure after the destruction of the city, the details need not concern us.

What does potentially concern us is the likelihood that a "pious fraud" of water to wine "magic" was involved in the cult. Such supposed "miracles" were wide-spread in the ancient world. Bonner reviews many of them and cites ancient literature on how water was changed to wine in various temples throughout the pagan world from Classical through Roman times.[4]

St. Paul, in writing to the congregation at Corinth, as well as in writing to the congregation at Rome (which was written from Corinth), avoids talking about miracles. Instead, he emphasized faith, morality, humility, and a willingness to get along with everyone who observed the canons of morality. Presumably he found that the good news about the love of God for all people was powerful enough to counter the pagan bad news about gods of terror and retribution, even if the bad news was accompanied by cheap magic tricks.

In spite of this, cheap magic tricks can influence the credulous, and this may be why the Apostle John chose to tell the people that Jesus could also turn water into wine, and not in the suspect way that the mystery religions did the trick. When Jesus turned water into wine, it was not in a secret temple rite, but at a public wedding party, in a way that could not possibly have involved sleight of hand. Not only did John feel that the story of the public miracle should be told, but he identified it as the very first sign of Jesus' mission as messiah (John 2:1-12a).

---

1 Landon, p. 47.

2 Bonner.

3 For versions of the Kotyto story, with sources, and some speculations on the nature of the cult worship, see Larson, pp. 138-139. Also see Steiner, p. 405.

4 Bonner, pp. 371-372.

A CHARACTER OF LEGEND

We need to start with a clarification of terms. In ancient Greece, "cynic" had a little different meaning than it has in English today. The ancient Greek "Cynic" was a philosophical seeker after truth who believed that the true life was the independent life. When we say, "independent," we mean independent of everything. The real Cynic forsook any possessions that were not absolutely necessary, forsook earthly pleasures that might compromise his independence, forsook family, friends, and national loyalties. The Cynic had a negative view of all of these things, and that negative view is the source of the modern English definition of "cynic."

The Cynic school was founded by Antisthenes, who, along with Plato, was a student of Socrates. Plato and Antisthenes had learned entirely different things from Socrates. Plato had learned from Socrates to value the intellectual life, a search for intellectual truth, and he saw that the highest reality is a "heavenly" world of ideas and ideals. In contrast, Antisthenes valued a life lived independently of all outside influence, and saw the highest form of life to be free from attachment to earthly pleasures and possessions. Intellectual understanding of the world was not high on Antisthenes' list of priorities.

Both of these points of view could be seen as consistent with the teaching of Jesus, and both have influenced the history of Christian theology. In the early middle ages, the Neo-Platonists claimed to draw their strange teachings from Plato combined with Jesus, and the anchorites who chose to live alone in desert caves or lived out their lives on top of pillars, as did St. Simon Stylites, drew their strange teachings from the Cynics combined with Jesus. Today we would judge that both points of view, when taken to their extreme, lead to absurd untruth.

Because he rejected interpersonal relationships that might compromise his personal independence, the Cynic philosopher might be rude to other people, and he certainly would not take other people's feelings into consideration when deciding what to do. Of course, there are people who are simply rude and unfeeling who never dignify their actions with a philosophical justification, but the Cynic heritage in Corinth may have influenced how some Corinthians behaved.

So, when St. Paul affirmed that the individual is free to eat whatever is set before him (a point of view which a Cynic would also affirm), but then advised that the individual should refrain from eating if the act of eating would harm the beliefs of a neighbor (and here the Cynic would strongly disagree with St. Paul), he might have been specifically arguing against the Cynics. (I Cor 10:23-30.)

It is also possible that at the supposed celebration of the "Lord's Supper," Cynic philosophy was partly responsible for the practice of some people eating more than they needed while others went hungry (I Cor 11:21). In this case, it certainly was not the "Lord's Supper," and it was not even a "fellowship supper," but the behavior of those who ignored the hungry was consistent with a popular understanding of Cynic philosophy.

Diogenes of Sinope was a student of Antisthenes. History records a number of ancient Greeks named Diogenes, but Diogenes of Sinope became a legend in Corinth because of his strange life and teaching.

Diogenes took the teaching of Antisthenes to the extreme. He was born a free Athenian, and it was as a free youth that he studied Cynicism. He was then taken prisoner by pirates, and was sold as a slave in Corinth. Through it all, he claimed that his personal situation made no difference, because he was "free" in every situation.[1] We know little for certain about the life of Diogenes, but many stories were told and retold about him so that he became a legendary figure, and it is the legend that interests us, because by the time of St. Paul, about 300 years after Diogenes, the legends were what mattered.

Did Diogenes still "matter" in the Corinth of St. Paul? We have a Cynic sarcophagus found in Palermo, Italy, that has been dated in the late 200s, CE.[2] The Palermo sarcophagus has a carved scene showing a man and wife getting married along with a musician and a teacher. On both sides of this group of folks are Cynic devotees pointing their fingers at them. Art historian W. Amelung comments, "Indeed we know that [Cynics] ridiculed marriage, science, and the musical arts. All these we see before us in the middle group . . . over whose quiet dignity and secluded life the chorus of Cynics outside intones its noisy parabasis." Amlung also relates this to St. Augustine's complaints about Cynics.[3]

If Cynic teaching was powerful enough in the late third century (150 years after St. Paul) to cause a follower to commission a sarcophagus with a Cynic theme, then it was probably also current in the time of St. Paul. (What are we to say about the irony of a follower of the Cynics caring to commission an expensive carved sarcophagus?)

Of course, Palermo, Italy, was far away from Corinth, so maybe Cynicism was not a factor in the life of St. Paul's Corinth, but there is also a somewhat similar (but less elaborate) sarcophagus carving that was found in Sardis, one of sites of the seven churches of Revelation in modern Turkey.[4] Thus Corinth is "surrounded" by Cynic monuments.

Monuments don't speak. Maybe we misunderstand them. But we also have writings showing that the legend of Diogenes remained influential. A little more than a hundred years after St. Paul, Lucian of Samosata wrote Dialogues of the Dead in which Diogenes and other Cynics played a central role, making it obvious that all of the accomplishments and honors civilized society bestows on us will be worthless in the world of death. (Diogenes was still influential 1,500 years later. Several writers in the seventeenth century found the independence of Diogenes attractive and followed Lucian's example using him to highlight the silliness of many social customs.[5])

Furthermore, Diogenes was one of those strange characters who would be remembered, and even admired by certain people simply because he was unusual. The stories we have tell us that he lived in a big pot or jar, that he always had a dog, and that he consciously violated social codes by doing in public what is normally private. In particular, he urinated and defecated in public.

St. Paul taught that instead of seeking "freedom," we should seek ways to be obedient to God: "Obeying the commandments of God is everything." (I Cor 7:19b); "For though I am free with respect to all, I have made myself a slave to all, so that I might win more of them." (I Cor 9:19). St. Paul was certainly not an admirer of Diogenes.

If we want to understand the atmosphere of St. Paul's Corinth, we should understand Diogenes, and it may be worthwhile to consider a Christian response to Cynicism. After all, it is still an intellectual option for some people in our own time, especially some "idealistic" young people. In fact, many people have a hard time distinguishing the sense of virtuous independence of the Cynics and the teachings of the Hebrew prophets and of Jesus.

As an example, poet William Blake, in "The Marriage of Heaven and Hell," wrote: "I also asked Isaiah what made him go naked and barefoot for three years? He answered, the same that made our friend Diogenes the Grecian." The reference is to Isaiah 20, especially verses 2 and 3. When we think about the entire chapter, we understand that there is little comparison between the enacted prophecy/parable of Isaiah and the expression of contempt for society that Diogenes showed.

As another example, consider Matthew 9:19-22: "A scribe then approached and said, 'Teacher, I will follow you wherever you go.' And Jesus said to him, 'Foxes have holes and birds of the air have nests, but the Son of Man has nowhere to lay his head.' Another of his disciples said to him, 'Lord, first let me go and bury my father.' But Jesus said to him, 'Follow me, and let the dead bury their own dead.'" This passage, which has been generally interpreted as demonstrating a concern for preparation for the eminent end of the world, sounds a lot like Cynic philosophy, showing no concern for ordinary worldly concerns. However, the Cynics taught that "virtue," and therefore happiness, was the goal of avoiding worldly concerns. Unlike the Cynics, Jesus did not teach his disciples to leave society in a search for happiness, but to redeem society. Jesus did not reject civilization, but had "nowhere to lay his head" because he was always on the move, trying to reach and redeem as many people as possible.

Compare this with another passage, Matthew 11:16-19: "But to what will I compare this generation? It is like children sitting in the marketplaces and calling to one another, 'We played the flute for you, and you did not dance; we wailed, and you did not mourn.' For John came neither eating nor drinking, and they say, 'He has a demon'; the Son of Man came eating and drinking, and they say, 'Look, a glutton and a drunkard, a friend of tax collectors and sinners!' Yet wisdom is vindicated by her deeds." This quotation demonstrates that among Jesus' acquaintances and associates, if anyone had a Cynic-like reputation, it was John the Baptist, not Jesus. A story that counters the legends of Diogenes, is the story that precedes this statement of Jesus, when Jesus tells John's disciples that he has been healing the sick and preaching good news to the poor. No Cynic would have seen these tasks as worth their time.

---

1 Stace, pp. 158-160.

2 Amelung, pp. 294-295.

3 Amelung, p. 296.

4 Amellung, p. 293.

5 Mazella.

COMMUNITY OF KNOWLEDGE

One of the eternal questions of philosophy is about the nature of knowledge. What do we know? Under what circumstances do we know? How do we know that we know?

In St. Paul's world, these questions were addressed most explicitly by the Platonists (not just Plato, but the following generations of followers and interpreters of Plato) and the Stoics. These two groups engaged in much philosophical debate, but they really agreed about the essence of "knowledge." For example, John Dillon, a historian of philosophy, quotes Philo as saying knowledge is "sure and certain conception which cannot be shaken by argument." Dillon goes on to say that this is a Stoic definition which "presupposes the whole Stoic theory of knowledge."[1]

This may sound too abstract to have any implications for the ordinary person of faith, but St. Paul seems to have recognized that it does have consequences for our lives.

First, a note about Philo. He was a contemporary of St. Paul, although probably 20 or 30 years older. He was a devout Jew who had a good Greek education. The purpose of his writings was to show that the faith taught by Moses in the Pentatuch was consistent with Plato's philosophy. As a matter of fact, he went beyond saying that Moses and Plato were consistent. He says that the teaching of Moses became the basis for the teaching of Plato, because Plato was influenced by Pythagoras (of mathematical fame), and Pythagoras, as a young man, had spent time in Palestine "consorting with the descendants of Môchos the prophet and philosopher." Dillon comments, "This Môchos . . . does sound suspiciously like a garbled form of Moses himself. . . . The philosophy which we find Moses expounding . . . . bears an extraordinary resemblance to Stoicized Platonism."[2]

There was a great deal of intellectual exchange around the empire, but it seems unlikely that St. Paul was aware of Philo of Alexanderia. We quote Philo's definition of "knowledge" simply because it represents a wide-spread notion in the time of St. Paul. Platonism and Stoicism were popular philosophies studied by educated people throughout the empire.

Let's look at another early Platonist who lived about a generation before St. Paul. Varro said,

> God is the soul of the universe, and this
> universe is God. But just as a wise man,
> though consisting of body and mind, is
> called wise because of his mind, so the
> universe is called God because of its
> mind, though it likewise consists of mind
> and body.[3]

Both Philo and Varro emphasize the individual, and in doing so, they represent the consensus of Greek philosophy. In Greek philosophy, knowledge was seen as something the individual possessed. It was firm and became the basis for action. Likewise, wisdom was seen as highly individualized, the essential gift of God. Not only are they individual, but they are objective and unchangeable. Knowledge and wisdom are the essence of God.

Note that the Platonists and Stoics (and educated first century people generally) had abandoned the old pantheon, and believed in one God. They debated the nature of this God, and some of them might have accepted initiation into a mystery religion as we might accept initiation into a civic club, but they were convinced that there is only one God. This belief is what led educated people to participate in the life of a synagogue, even though they didn't convert to Judaism, and it later led them to join the Christian community.

Let's think about "knowledge" and "wisdom" as being fixed in the mind of God, and therefore unchangeable. This was Plato's essential doctrine. He taught that for everything we encounter on "earth," there is a perfect prototype (Plato called it an "idea") in "heaven." We can realize how familiar Plato's doctrine was when we consider that the biographer of ancient philosophers, Diogenes Laertius (not Diogenes the Cynic) included this in his account of Diogenes the Cynic:

> As Plato was conversing about ideas and using the nouns "tablehood" and "cuphood," Diogenes said, "Table and cup I see, but your tablehood and cuphood, Plato, I cannot see at all." That's readily accounted for," said Plato, "for you have eyes to see the visible table and cup, but not the understanding by which ideal tablehood and cuphood are discerned.[4]

According to Platonic philosophy, every table we see is modeled after a perfect, ideal table in the mind of God. Likewise, every person we see is modeled after a perfect, ideal person in the mind of God. Furthermore, when we find a wise person, that person's wisdom is modeled after perfect, ideal wisdom in the mind of God.

Of course, "knowledge" and "wisdom" really are individual qualities. We tend to see them that way even if we haven't been schooled in Greek philosophy. Furthermore, the biblical book of Proverbs clearly presents "wisdom" as a quality the individual should strive to attain.

St. Paul, however, saw a problem with the fixed categories of Greek philosophy. An over-emphasis on individual wisdom and individual knowledge separates us from one another. That is why he began his first letter to the Corinthians with a complaint about their emphasis on knowledge and wisdom, saying (facetiously) that he, himself, had no wisdom.

We can see that this was not just a passing comment, but was basic to his analysis of the Corinthian problem, because he brought it up again in the great "love chapter": "For now we know in part . . . but when the perfect comes, the imperfect will pass away. . . . faith, hope and love abide."

This is revolutionary! Knowledge does not last forever. Wisdom does not last forever. Only faith, hope and love last forever! Only faith, hope and love are in the mind of God! Not only that, but our "knowledge" is imperfect. This leads to part of his over-all concern with the Corinthians, which is that they are not cooperating and working together for their mutual good and for the good of the kingdom of God. If our "knowledge" is imperfect, then we must work together to pool our knowledge so that it might be better than any person's individual knowledge.

This, of course represents the basis for our modern society. It is the basis for modern science, modern engineering, modern commerce, modern government, everything. Today we cannot assume that anyone is fully knowledgeable or fully wise. Our entire educational establishment is based on the assumption that we need to specialize and then cooperate.

---

1 Dillon, p. 145.

2 Dillon, p. 143.

3 Dillon, p. 90.

4 Diogenes Laertius, p. 143.

The Lechaeum Road as it enters the city.

How Good is God?

Rabbi Harold Kushner phrased the question well: "Why do bad things happen to good people?"[1] Some thinkers consider that this is the basic question that all religions attempt to answer.

Traditional Greek religion answered the question in terms of self-seeking and rivalries among the various gods. The Trojan War that slaughtered so many people was the result of competition among the gods, when Aphrodite gave Helen of Troy to Paris as a reward (bribe?) for judging in her favor against Athena and Hera. The Greek gods were continually at cross-purposes with one another.

As far as we can tell, the popular mystery religions didn't offer an answer to the question of why bad things happen. Instead, they offered a way out, a form of what we might call "salvation." Persian Zoroastrianism had reduced the list of gods to two—a good one and an evil one—and Christians tended to accept this notion with modifications. The bad one, Satan, is not a god, but Satan is more powerful than us, and causes us a lot of trouble.

Philosophers, especially Cynics like Diogenes, taught that evil comes from inside of us, not from some god or devil. If we desire too much, we'll get into trouble. If we live simply and independently, everything will be all right. Of course, Jesus taught simple living, but Jesus also worked hard to cleanse people of their demons. According to the teaching of Jesus, not all evil is the result of our bad decisions.

St. Paul would not have been worth much as a religious teacher if he had not had something to say about the bad things that happen, and with the variety of explanations of why bad things happen, whatever St. Paul said would be a challenge to someone else's teaching. Of course he taught that the venality of the traditional ancient gods was false and that the mystery religions were empty, but there was more to be said.

A "new" school of thought was increasing in popularity. Like the mystery religions, it taught that if you just understood "secret stuff," you could overcome evil. In the time after St. Paul, this teaching was developed by various thinkers who placed their own stamp on the "faith," so that in the second century we find the early Christian theologians wrestling with competing schools of "secret" thought. One of the second century teachers of "secrets" was named Valentinus. Another was Basilides.[2] They disagreed with each other on details, but their themes were similar, and they thought that what they were teaching was consistent with the Christian faith.

As a group, these teachers are called "Gnostics," and their teaching is called "Gnosticism." It is unbelievably complicated, and some modern scholars question whether it is really useful to group all of the diverse forms of Gnosticism under one label. We'll not worry about that. The important point for us is that although the Gnostic ideas were not fully developed in St. Paul's day, they seem to have been "in the atmosphere."

The key to the Gnostic way of explaining evil is that they taught that God is evil, or at least imperfect and corrupt. When they say this, they are not speaking about any of the pagan gods. They are speaking of the God who created the world. Why would they say that? The answer goes back to the Greek philosophers who taught 300 and 400 years before St. Paul. The philosophers taught that "perfection" is static. If you make a perfect statue (maybe a statue of Zeus) it would just stand there. Likewise, the "perfect" god would just stand there.

Now it gets strange. If you believe that the philosophers taught the truth and that the Bible (or Torah) teaches the truth, you might look for ways to harmonize them. If perfection is static, then the one God, who is perfect, will not "do" anything. So how does the world get created? Gnostics came up with the notion that even though "God" is static, "God" sent out rays of perfection that coagulated into a lesser "God," and that "God" likewise sent out rays of perfection, making an even lesser "God," and this happened several times until "Jehovah" was made. "Jehovah" was far enough removed from the one "God" who started it all so that "Jehovah" was no longer static, and could actually do something, so "Jehovah" created the world.

However, because "Jehovah" was several cycles removed from perfection, "Jehovah" wasn't really perfect. (Have you ever photocopied a photocopy, then photocopied that photocopy, etc.? It doesn't take many cycles before the original is unrecognizable.) Therefore, the world that "Jehovah" made is, at best, imperfect, and at worst, evil.

Remind yourself that these ideas were not systematized when St. Paul was writing, but they were part of the intellectual atmosphere. These strange Gnostic ideas may have, at least subconsciously, prompted some of St. Paul's greatest writings, and the writings probably reflect the sermons he was preaching. Consider this: "If God is for us, who is against us? . . . Who will separate us from the love of Christ? . . . Neither death, nor life, nor angels, nor rulers, nor things present, no things to come, nor powers, nor height, nor depth, nor anything else in all creation will be able to separate us from the love of God in Christ Jesus our Lord." (from Romans 8:31-39.) St. Paul wrote this while he was living in Corinth. Certainly he was also teaching this to the Corinthian congregation. This is a teaching about a good God who controls all of the "powers" and everything else. The Father of Jesus Christ is certainly not the limited, imperfect god of the Gnostics.

"Gnosis" is the Greek word for "knowledge." Certainly some of the members of the Corinthian congregation were proud of their philosophical knowledge. Perhaps others thought that they had "secret knowledge" that explained the ways of God. St. Paul was speaking both to the philosophers and to the Gnostics when he wrote to them, "Now I know only in part. Then I will know fully, even as I have been fully known." (I Cor 13:12b)

St. Paul clearly felt that the world is not bad. Bad things happen, but God gives us "weapons of righteousness." (II Cor 6:7, a theme that is elaborated in Ephesians 6:10-20.) There are evil forces in the cosmos, but with God's help we can endure and overcome, so "we entreat you on behalf of Christ, be reconciled to God." (II Cor 5:20). If "God" was the corrupt "God" of the Gnostics, the idea of reconciliation would be absurd.

What about the flesh? Doesn't St. Paul teach that sin is imbedded in our flesh? If the flesh is bad, doesn't that indicate that the world is bad? These questions come from a superficial reading of St. Paul, a careful teacher who makes subtle distinctions. Volumes have been written on this, and in this small essay we can only point to a hint of St. Paul's thought: "The body is meant not for fornication but for the Lord, and the Lord for the body. And God raised the Lord and will also raise us by his power." (I Cor 6:13b-14) No statement could be less Gnostic than this.

The world is not bad, but it is not the best, and this has led some, even in our day, to suggest that followers of Jesus have no responsibility for the world. This is a semi-gnostic idea that St. Paul rejects when he teaches about morality in I Corinthians, and even when he urges the congregation to give generously in II Corinthians 8 and 9. We are responsible for one another.

St. Paul looks forward to heaven, but doesn't expect to get there by the power of secret knowledge. He will get there by the power of God who is good: "Even though our outer nature is wasting away, our inner nature is being renewed day by day. . . for what can be seen is temporary, but what cannot be seen is eternal . . . He who has prepared us for this very thing [heaven] is God, who has given us the Spirit as a guarantee." (II Cor 4:16-5:5)

Remember that the Gnostics taught that God made a lesser God, who made a lesser God, etc. Imbedded in this is the notion that there are several heavens. We have a hard time realizing that in the time of St. Paul, everyone believed in multiple heavens. It was not only a religious or philosophical idea. The best astronomical science of the day taught that there were several heavens. Claudius Ptolemy, who lived after St. Paul, developed ideas of multiple heavens that had first been proposed as far back as Plato. This was a way of explaining the movement of the planets: the cosmos is a series of crystal spheres around the earth, the stars, including the planets, are on the surface of one or another of these spheres. The spheres rotate around the earth in different directions, providing the planetary movement that we see.[3] Each of these spheres is a heaven, and each of the stars is an angel.

So it is that St. Paul claimed to have seen the third of these spheres, and was overwhelmed by its glory. (II Cor 12:2-5. No one ever doubted that he was speaking about himself.) The casual reader might think that St. Paul was agreeing with the Gnostic notion of several heavens. Not so. The Gnostics were the ones who agreed: they accepted the universal understanding of the cosmos at that time.

The Gnostics tried to have the last word. Valentinus took St. Paul's writings, turned them around, and claimed that St. Paul was the original Gnostic, because he talked about "secret" knowledge. Pagels studied these claims and concluded that "we can account for allegedly 'gnostic terminology' in Paul's letters if we assume that Paul's theological language is appropriated and developed subsequently by the Vanentinians (and other gnostics) into a technical theological vocabulary."[4]

Was St. Paul really aware of the Gnostic challenge? We repeat that their ideas were in their infancy during his time, so maybe St. Paul wasn't specifically responding to them, but his clear thinking on questions of God, love, and goodness pro-

vided a basis for later generations who were called on to respond to the accusation that God is really bad.

---

1 Kushner.

2 Samples of Valentinus and Basilides can be found in any edition of Stevenson.

3 This complicated system is explained in some detail by Kuhn, pp. 55 -73.

4 Pagels, p. 163.

Plato the
philosopher

LOGIC OF GODDESSES

"And do you really tell Truth?"
"I do."
"Do you, by Vesta?"
"Yes, and by Neptune too."
"What Neptune, do you mean the God of the Sea?"
"Ay, and t'other Neptune too, if there be any other."
          —Aristophanes, *Plutus, The God of Riches.*[1]

". . . this was a joke on the Athenians, for worshipping Neptune under different names, as the Sea Neptune, the Horseman Neptune, etc."[2]

191

Aristophanes was a contemporary of Plato, possibly acquainted with him, and possibly a friend. In writing these lines, he displayed an early awareness of the "law of noncontradiction" which would be systematized by Plato's student, Aristotle. We can understand the joke, but apparently it "went over the heads" of most people in the ancient world.

It was extremely common for one god to be worshipped in two different temples, each temple celebrating a different aspect, or power of that god. This leads to the question, was one god being worshipped, or two? Furthermore, if two gods shared a power, were they two or one? This gets confusing. Residents of Corinth were not only willing to worship Kore as goddess of the underworld and Isis as goddess of the underworld, but sometimes said that Kore and Isis were the same, even though they had different temples and different liturgies. Sometimes Kore and her mother, Demeter were considered to be the same. Isis was apparently sometimes considered to be two different goddesses, because on the Acrocorinth there were two temples to Isis under different names. Sometimes Isis, goddess of the underworld, was considered the same as Aphrodite, goddess of love. Sometimes Kore, the maiden (or virgin) was considered the same as Aphrodite, definitely not a virgin (although sometimes Aphrodite was seen as a virgin).

This amazing confusion was equally apparent among the male gods. Dionysus was sometimes considered the same as Apollo, but sometimes not. On the Acrocorinth, there were two temples to European Serapis who may or may not have been the same as the Egyptian Osiris. (One of the Serapis temples was apparently Egyptian.)

This takes us back to Aristotle. Aristotle's book of Logic was revolutionary. Many of the principles he taught were not new, but he organized these principles and gave names to their procedures. Aristotle considered the most basic logical "truth" to be what we know as the "law of noncontradiction." Aristotle explained it this way: "The same attribute cannot belong and not belong to the same subject and in the same respect."[3] In other words, if the animal on the hill is a goat, it is not a sheep, and if it is a sheep, it is not a goat.[4]

Aristotle taught that the law of noncontradiction is self-evident, and most of us would agree. It is so much a part of our daily thought process that we can't imagine living in a confused world in which clearly different things are considered to be the same thing, while at the same time also admitting that they are different. This may sound like "goblty-gook," but it describes the thought process of many people in St. Paul's Corinth.[5] We know that there is always a lag between a scientific or academic discovery and the public understanding and using it. One of the problems of modern society is reducing this lag time so that, for example, improved medical procedures are actually used by the physicians who treat us. In the ancient world, the lag time could be quite long. Aristotle had written his Logic almost 400 years before St. Paul visited Corinth, but many people still had not heard about it and did not understand it. Clearly many people did not consider the law of noncontradiction to apply to goddesses and gods. With all of the confusion among them, how many gods and goddesses were there? Only Zeus knows.

Of course, some people understood Aristotle's logical point of view. We assume that these tended to be educated folks who liked to display their education and had contempt for the common folks who lacked understanding of Aristotle's teaching about logic and rhetoric. Apparently the congregation St. Paul organized in Corinth included both kinds of people, and this would have been part of the reason for tension in the congregation. (This is not to imply that it is impossible to have a cohesive congregation composed of members of various socioeconomic classes. We know, for example, that the congregation in Phillipi included Lydia, presumably a refined businesswoman along with the keeper of the jail, presumably a rough-living, rough-talking, uneducated man [Acts 16:11-40], and based on St. Paul's letter to the Phillipians, the congregation appears to have been successful.)

When St. Paul was giving advice about food offered to idols, he said, "there is one God, the Father, from whom are all things and for whom we exist, and one Lord, Jesus Christ, through whom are all things and through whom we exist. It is not everyone, however, who has this knowledge." (I Cor 8:6-7). He was asserting the principle of noncontradiction as a basic truth of theology even as he wrestled with the relationship between the Father and the Son.

St. Paul was clearly an educated person. His letters show that he understood and used both Jewish and Aristotelian principles of rhetoric and logic,[6] but he apparently didn't flaunt his education in his daily contacts in the city. This is not to say that he never showed his education, he just didn't "show off" his education. This gives us an insight into his comment, "I have become all things to all people," (I Cor. 9:22) a comment that, when quoted out of context, sounds arrogant. Certainly no one can be "all things" in a literal sense, and St. Paul recognized that fact when he formulated his lists of "spiritual gifts" (Rom. 12:6-8, I Cor. 12:28-30, Eph. 4:11-12), but he could talk about Jewish concerns with Jews and Gentile concerns with Gentiles, educated concerns with the educated, and working-class concerns with the working-class. Thus, presumably educated people such as Gaius, Stephanus and Erastus were attracted to the congregation, along with unnamed working people and slaves.

When we travel the world today, we find that some in some cultures, if a person has education, they are expected to "flaunt" it, while in other cultures (particularly the U.S.A.) it is considered bad form to make a show of one's education. It is easy to assume that people in Corinth expected an educated person to "act educated." It seems likely that Apollos (I Cor. 1:12), who came to the congregation after St. Paul left, was educated in Aristotelian rhetoric, and showed it off. Some in the congregation preferred his sophisticated style, while others missed St. Paul's "common" approach.

When it was necessary, St. Paul could show his education, and it was necessary in discussing the resurrection, a topic of importance to the death-conscious Corinthians. Aristotle had defined and analyzed extensively the logical procedure which he named the "syllogism" and St. Paul understood the basic ideas behind syllogistic logic. I Cor. 15:12-19 is a series of syllogistic arguments, starting with this one (which happens to use the Aristotelian "third form"[7]):

1. Christ is raised from the dead.
2. Christ is someone.
3. Someone is raised from the dead.

And the argument proceeds from there using Aristotle all the way.[8]

Aristotle also taught that if you make a statement about something, you can describe that thing in terms of ten categories, such as quality, quantity, place and time. In I Cor. 15:20-28, St. Paul carries the argument about the resurrection through a time sequence in which he displays an awareness of "categories," such as "first fruits."

Greek philosophy was very interested in change, and Aristotle taught that any change involves four "causes." In the modern world, we no longer recognize Aristotle's "causes" as a valid description of change, but St. Paul apparently knew that Aristotle's fourth "cause" had to do with the purpose of the change, so St. Paul specifies the ultimate purpose of the change that took place when Christ was raised: "For he must reign until he has put all enemies under his feet. The last enemy to be destroyed is death." (I Cor. 15:25-26.)

I Cor. 15:35-41 brings us back to the law of non-contradiction. St. Paul argues that bodies that serve different purposes are different, so the resurrection body is not the same as the earthly body. In other words, he is not talking about Kore or Isis or any of those divinities. Christ is unique and so are we. Christ's resurrection body is unique, and so are ours.[9]

This short discussion is not intended to be an exhaustive treatise on St. Paul's use of Aristotle's logic,[10] but simply to point out that (a) unlike the goddesses and gods of the Acrocorinth and Agora, logic could be applied to Christ, and (b) St. Paul had the background to apply the logic. Some have said that St. Paul really wasn't very well educated, and that his letters show no real sign of what would have been called "education," but his consistent use of Aristotelian categories and procedures when it is appropriate suggest that he was indeed educated, simply refusing to "show off."

---

1 Aristophenes, *Plutus (403-408)*, p. 40.

2 From a footnote by Fielding and Young, p. 40, commenting on the *Plutus* dialogue.

3 Aristotle, *Metaphysics*, Bk IV, ch 3, 1005b(18). Tr. Ross, p. 524.

4 A good summary of Aristotle's teachings can be found in Russell. Note that not all logic was Aristotlian. The stoics had their own canons of logic, and St. Paul does not appear to have used any of their canons or categories. See Reesor, 1965, and her follow-up article, 1972, for a summary of stoic logic.

5 In modern mathematics, we sometimes find that mathematical structures that seem different are really the same ("isomorphic"). For example, vector spaces and matrices appear to be different, but are not. However, the devotees of ancient Greek goddesses were not modern mathematicians.

6 See the essay "How Was St. Paul Educated?"

7 This is not to suggest that St. Paul would have been able to tell you that it was a "third form" argument. The point is simply that St. Paul was comfortable with syllogistic reasoning.

8 St. Paul was not a flawless logician. Here we ignore St. Paul's qualification in verse 12 that Christ is "preached" or "proclaimed" as having been raised from the dead, a qualification that flaws the logic. Our purpose is not to analyze the logical validity of the argument, but to indicate that the argument is based on Aristotle's principles.

9 For more comment on the resurrection body, see the essay, "Death Takes No Holiday."

10 His arguments were not always Aristotelian. Sometimes he used rabbinic arguments. We mention them in another essay, "How Was St. Paul Educated?"

DISUNITY IN CORINTH

Clearly there was severe disunity in the Corinthian congregation—that was the problem St. Paul was addressing in his letters. Furthermore, disunity seems to have been a persistent problem within that congregation, because St. Clement of Rome, writing to the Corinthians about 50 years after St. Paul's visit, addressed the same problem. St. Clement opened his letter with extravagant compliments: "Who has not admired the sobriety and Christian gentleness of your piety? . . . you did all things without respect of persons and walked in the laws of God . . . and you were all humble-minded and in no wise arrogant . . . you had an insatiable desire to do good . . ."

But this praise was in preparation for a severe tongue-lashing: "All glory and enlargement was given to you . . . From this arose jealousy and envy, strife and sedition, persecution and disorder, war and captivity. Thus 'the worthless' rose up 'against those who were in honor,' those of no reputation against the renowned, the foolish against the prudent, the 'young against the old.' For this cause righteousness and peace are far removed, while each deserts the fear of God and the eye of faith in him has gown dim, and men walk neither in the ordinances of his commandments nor use their citizenship worthily of Christ, but each goes according to the lusts of his wicked heart, and has revived the unrighteousness and impious envy, by which also 'death comes into the world.'"[1]

Every pastor knows that all congregations have their problems, so it is not surprising that there were problems in the Corinthian congregation, even though the problems may have been a bit more severe than most. The question for us, as we seek to understand the people of Corinth, is whether the disunity can help us understand these people.

On the surface St. Paul seems to be attempting to "patch up" several fractures in the congregation: party spirit (I Cor. 1:12, etc.), disagreements about sexual behavior (I Cor. 5, etc.), lawsuits within the congregation (I Cor. 6), attitude toward idolatry (I Cor. 8, etc.), the Lord's Supper (I Cor. 11:17, etc.), and speaking in tongues (I Cor. 12-14). Perhaps these are all symptoms of a more basic split.

Corinth, itself, was a disunited city. Some residents remembered the "old" Corinth and honored the remnants of the once proud city that had been destroyed 200 years before St. Paul's visit. Many residents were from families "imported" to the city by Julius Caesar when he reestablished it, a hundred years before St. Paul's visit. We don't know exactly where these "imported" families came from, but many were apparently freed slaves brought in from various locations around the Empire. They would have brought several cultures to the city.

Some of them would have been Jews, bringing the Jewish religion and culture. This could have been why Priscila and Aquila (probably along with others) were attracted to Corinth after the emperor Claudius had ordered all Jews to leave Rome. (Acts 18:2.)

Because it was a city of "freedmen," they respected manual labor, in contrast to most cities in the Empire where wealthy people did not work and disdained anyone who did work. Also, there was work available in this industrial port city. No doubt other freedmen were attracted to Corinth, further complicating the cultural identity of Roman Corinth.

In addition to freedmen, there were slaves, for in the Roman Empire slaves functioned at all levels in the economy, being assigned to back-breaking labor and also to trusted offices in the administration of public affairs.

Of course there were educated people too, and there were freedmen and children of freedmen and slaves and children of slaves who were naturally attuned toward intellectual pursuits. We can imagine that they felt isolated, as intellectuals often do in communities that are far away from the intellectual centers where the great universities are located. As far as we know, there were no universities (or schools of philosophy) in Roman Corinth.

We can mention other social factors (which will be mentioned in other essays in this book), but the point is that Roman Corinth was a fractured society. St. Paul came there and attracted followers from many segments of the society, then Apollos came and attracted another kind of people, and likely other evangelists (possibly including Simon Peter) came and attracted more folks. It's something of a miracle that the congregation held together at all.

The congregation did hold together, and St. Paul was writing to the whole congregation, not to a faction within it.

Now we return to our first question: was there a basic problem underlying the disputes within the congregation? Probably so. If so, was it a theological dispute? Probably not. If not, what was the nature of the dispute?

We turn to a perceptive academic article by L. L. Welborn.[2] He notes that John Calvin recognized that the Corinthian problem is not a doctrinal problem. If it were, St. Paul would have taken sides in the dispute, but he didn't. St. Paul's arguments in I Corinthians are much different from his arguments against false teaching in Galatians and Philippians.[3] Welborn examines St. Paul's Greek vocabulary in the first four chapters of I Cor. and finds "political" words throughout the passage,[4] and he finds that the slogans used by the factions ("of Paul," "of Apollos," etc.) are similar to the political graffiti we find in the ruins of Pompeii and generally typical of what we know of Roman party politics.[5]

What, then, is the basis of the "party spirit" within the Corinthian congregation? Perhaps it is a general tendency to argue loudly about concerns, and we shouldn't discount it. Usually there is more than one cause for a phenomenon, and the argumentativeness modeled by Sophist philosophers can be a cause here.[6] Maybe there was a "hidden" theological split symbolized by the notion of wisdom.[7] We repeat, there is usually more than one cause for a phenomenon.

Welborn suggests that there is a more important cause: social and economic inequality. We see this especially in the controversy over the Lord's Supper (I Cor. 11:17-34) when the apparently wealthy dined well and the apparently poor were left wanting, but Welborn says a concern about social inequality shows up throughout I Corinthians and is also a theme of much ancient Greek political writing. For example, he quotes Aristotle, "Party strife is everywhere due to inequality."[8] Drawing on his study of the way Greek writers commonly used vocabulary, Welborn says that in I Cor. 1:26-31, when St. Paul refers to the "wise," etc., he is talking about "the rich," and when he refers to the "foolish," etc., he is talking about "the poor."[9] After quoting many Greek writers, Welborn says, "The absolute dichotomy they express corresponds to the wide gulf between the rich and the poor in the ancient economy."[10]

St. Paul, however, was no political revolutionary. He did not directly confront the wealthy and powerful in the congregation, but he attempted to reconcile the factions wherever possible. Of course, when he chastised the people for initiating lawsuits against one another, he chastised the wealthy, because the poor were not able to initiate lawsuits, but Welborn points out that the party of poor people would be led by wealthy patrons who wanted to enhance their status by having a large following, so St. Paul addresses "those whom he regards as the prime movers in faction, the social and political elite."[11]

On the matter of lawsuits, we, who live in a litigious era, might ask why it is not morally and ethically right to appeal to courts when there is injustice. St. Paul may have been so opposed to legal action because he knew the traditional teaching of Jesus that became part of Matthew's Gospel (17:15-17).

He also may have had in mind the fact that the Romans had once given the Jews authority to conduct their own courts, instead of going before pagan judges.[12]

This brief discussion neither summarizes nor settles all of the scholarly debates about the background and nature of Corinthian factionalism, but as we look around the ancient city, we need to keep in mind that the city influenced the people, as it does everywhere in every age.

---

1 Clement of Rome, pp. 9-15.

2 Welborn.

3 Welborn, p. 89.

4 Welborn, pp. 86-88.

5 Welborn, pp. 90-93.

6 Ven Kooten.

7 Grindheim.

8 Welborn, p. 94.

9 Welborn, p. 96.

10 Welborn, p. 97.

11 Welborn, p. 98.

12 Klausner, p. 18.

WHEN IS AN IDOL
NOT AN IDOL?

As we have said in another essay, ancient Corinth was a city of temples[1] and images of gods (Greeks called them "images," Jews called them "idols"). Travel writer Pausanias tells us about more than 50 statues of gods in the "metropolitan area" (Lechaeum, Cenchreae, Isthmea, Corinth, and on the Acrocorinth), and we know he missed some. For example, he does not tell us about an erotic marble statue of Aphrodite in the theatre district.[2] Pausanias not only catalogs the statues, he describes them in what seems to be reverential terms, telling us as much as he knows about them: their specific name, the history of the statue, the material from which it was crafted, and the sculptor. Each one seems to be an object of devotion. They are not simply decorative, and they don't seem to have been pigeon roosts. People actually worshipped them.

In the Roman Empire, the reason for religious idolatry was partly "patriotic," because Augustus and the emperors who followed him used traditional religion as a means of solidifying the empire under their rule. Michael Grant has said, "No one made greater use than Augustus of the traditional Roman religion in order to secure the acceptance of his regime. . . . and long after Christianity became Rome's official faith there were still nostalgic, aristocratic groups in the capital who cherished the traditional paganism as the core and origin of Roman power."[3]

However human attitudes are seldom the result of one motive. Apart from "patriotism," many people did find spiritual depth in the system of idols and animal sacrifices. Pausanias tells of a theological problem faced by some residents of Sycion, a town about seven miles from Corinth. There was a dispute as to whether to honor Heracles as a hero or as a god, and Pausanias tells us that "Even at the present day the Sicyonians, after slaying a lamb and burning the thighs upon the altar, eat some of the meat as part of a victim given to a god, while the rest they offer as to a hero."[4] There is a tantalizing lack of information here. We are curious about the differences in ritual between honoring a god and honoring a hero. Even so, the fact that a theological dispute led to such a compromise demonstrates that some folks took the sacrifice as more than an empty ritual.

Idolatry was one of the problems the members of the Corinthian congregation wanted advice about, and when we see the scope of idolatry in the city, we can understand why it was an issue. St. Paul divides his advice into two sections. First, he addresses the problem of sacrificial meat in I Cor. 8.

In addition to his catalog of "images," Pausanias describes about 32 temples in Corinth and its suburbs, and it is in these temples that animals were sacrificed. In the ancient world, when animals were slaughtered for meat, they were officially dedicated to one or another of the gods. The gods needed only certain portions of the animal, so what was left over was available for human consumption. The concept of providing food for the gods through sacrifice was common to all of the ancient cultures.[5]

It is interesting that in only one case does Pausanias mention Corinthian sacrifice. He tells us that in Isthmea, there was a temple to the Cyclopes where sacrifices were offered. This is not to imply that sacrifices were not offered in the other temples. The reader gets the impression that the reason for mentioning sacrifice to Cyclopes is not the sacrifice, but the fact that sacrifice is offered to Cyclopes, an unusual object of devotion. The Cyclopes were not part of the pantheon of gods but Corinth was a major port city, and sailors would be worried about being shipwrecked on an island inhabited by the vicious Cyclopes,[6] so before they set out from Corinth, they would make an offering, just in case.

Of course people made sacrificial offerings to Aphrodite, Apollo, and all the others.[7] Every day several hundred domestic animals were sacrificed in every Greek city and the meat was eaten in public ceremonies.[8] We get the impression that meat was otherwise unavailable. Ancient Greeks didn't pack a bologna sandwich for lunch.

In Corinth, the meat market seems to have been conveniently located behind a row of temples on the west side of the Agora. When St. Paul was there, each of the shops behind the temples had a water well, which could have been used for "refrigeration" of fresh meat. (During the reign of Nero these shops were closed and converted into bureaucratic office space.[9])

St. Paul faced a problem. What should the members of the Corinthian congregation eat? Should they keep kosher? Could they keep kosher? Should they become vegetarians? He chose the solution favored by educated people of his time.

The common opinion among educated people was that the ancient gods were simply superstition, and St. Paul agreed (I Cor 8). If the statues are not really gods, then the fact that the meat has been dedicated to these gods makes no difference. But not everyone was educated, and even among the educated, traces of superstition remained. What if you are eating with a sailor in Isthmea, and the sailor knows that the meat has been part of a sacrifice to the deadly Cyclopes? Should you eat it? St. Paul at this point becomes Ann Landers or Miss Manners. He says that you should not offend anyone when you exercise your freedom to eat.

There is another problem, however. All of this meat was eaten in pagan temples in conjunction with pagan liturgy. In I Cor. 8, St. Paul recognized that if the idols mean nothing, then the liturgy also means nothing, so you may as well eat, but in the second section on idolatry, in chapter 10, he hesitates . . . eat unless the liturgy involves immorality. Maybe you like meat flavored with juniper smoke. That means you have to go to a temple of Aphrodite for supper. Is there immorality in the liturgy of Aphrodite worship? St. Paul may not have been sure about this question, but he was sure that if there is immorality, we should stay away!

When he says, "Do not be idolaters as some of them were; as it is written, 'The people sat down to eat and drink and rose up to dance. We must not indulge in immorality as some of them did . . . ,'" (I Cor. 10:7-8) he is making direct reference to the wilderness wanderings of the Hebrews, but he is also applying it to the daily lives of those in the Corinthian congregation who may "sit down to eat and drink" in a pagan temple. Would they also "dance" (perhaps the ecstatic dance of Dionysian liturgies) or otherwise engage in immorality as a part of temple liturgy? As Robertson and Plummer say, "The apostle intimates, more plainly than before [that is, than in chapter 8], that the danger of actual idolatry is not so imaginary as the Corinthians in their enlightened emancipation supposed."[10]

---

1 See the essay, "City of Temples."

2 Williams, pp. 243-247.

33 Grant, Michael, pp. 181-182.

4 Pausanias, p. 299.

5 Gaster has basic background. For more detail on sacrifice, see Yerkes or Petropoulou.

6 Both Homer and Vergil described in gruesome detail the horrors of encountering the Cyclopes, so the stories were well known. Homer *Odyssey*, Bk. IX, pp. 122-135; Virgil, *Aeneid*, Bk. III, pp. 151-153.

7 Pausanias (p. 301) describes a sacrifice to Aphrodite in Sycion. For her, the wood for the fire had to be juniper.

8 Zaidman and Pantel, p. 30.

9 McDonald, pp. 43-44.

10 Robertson and Plummer, p. 203.

The Peirene Fountain. You would enter
one of the archways to draw water.

PAGAN SIN AND CHRISTIAN SIN

"Behold, God's Son is come unto this land . . . So changed in shape from God to Man, I walk again . . . [but Penthus] hath begun a war with God. He thrusteth me away from due drink offering, and when men pray, my name entreats not." – from the opening lines of *The Bacchae* by Euripides.[1]

In these lines from the tragic Greek drama about the followers of the god Bacchus, or Dionysus, the person referred to as "God's Son" who has come in the form of a man is none other than Dionysus. Dionysus is not Christ. Unlike Christ, Dionysus is concerned only with himself, as we see in his complaint that King Penthus doesn't believe in him. Penthus refuses to pray (or entreat) and refuses to make a drink offering to the god.

Throughout the drama, Dionysus is presented as a self-centered god. According to Dionysus, people commit "sin" when they refuse to honor the god by ritual, prayer, and offerings.

211

The plot of this play involves a conflict between King Penthus and Dionysus, with Penthus not being aware that Dionysus is real, is present, and is so offended that he will bring vengeance against Penthus. The women in the drama (including Penthus' own mother) are planning to go into the forest to hold a celebration in honor of Dionysus. Penthus is suspicious of what the women are planning, so he costumes himself as a devotee and follows them. When the women reach the site of the celebration, Penthus climbs a tree to see what is going on. The tree (controlled by Dionysus) bends down to reveal Penthus to the women. Under the spirit of the god (they are probably drunk) they think Penthus is a wild animal, and they physically rip his body apart. (We have pictures on ancient Greek vases showing followers of Dionysus ripping wild animals apart as part of their ritual.)

In the end, another sin is recognized, the sin of murder. The women who have murdered Penthus, even though they were doing it under the god's command, influence, and power, are exiled for their sin. Thus, the Greek tragedy is complete: no one escapes the capricious wrath of god.

One more aspect of sin is visible in this drama: the reason Penthus is intent on opposing Dionysus is his suspicion that the women are not going to the forest to worship, but to have a sexual orgy. As Penthus says, "Away into the loneliness now one steals forth, and now a second, maid or dame, where love lies waiting, not of God! The flame, they say, of Bacchios wraps them. Bacchios! Nay, 'tis more to Aphrodite that they pray."[2]

Another play by Euripides, *Hippolytus*, shows us the same range of sin. The opening speech in that play is spoken by

Aphrodite: "Wheresoe'er from Pontus to the far Red West men dwell, and see the glad day-star, and worship Me, the pious heart I bless, and wreck that life that lives in stubbornness. For that there is, even in a great God's mind, that hungereth for the praise of human kind."[3] The problem here is a clash between two goddesses, Aphrodite and Artemis. It is impossible to worship both of them, because Artemis honors virginity, and Aphrodite honors promiscuity.

In this drama, the young man, Hippolytus, has decided to live according to the dictates of Artemis, and Aphrodite is angry about his "sinful decision," therefore she causes the stepmother of Hippolytus to lust after him. It would be sinful for Hippolytus and his stepmother, Phaedra, to consummate a relationship, and so the clash of sins leads to tragedy.

According to the pagan world-view, there is redemption, but it is difficult because the gods are reluctant to accept repentance. In *Hippolytus*, a guide and hunting companion to the young man prays that Aphrodite might forgive the youthful pride of Hippolytus, saying, "Gods should be gentler and more wise than men."[4] The stern goddess of "love" spurns this prayer. In *The Bacchae*, the father of King Pentheus encourages him to honor the god even if he doesn't believe in him: "Grant that this God be naught, yet let that Naught be Somewhat in thy mouth; Lie boldly, and say He is!"[5] The pagan theology was a theology of legalism: make the right ritual offerings and everything will be all right.

Of course, Euripides lived centuries before St. Paul, but his dramas were based on enduring mythological stories, and we can safely assume that these stories were still told in St. Paul's time. (Ovid wrote about Phaedra and Hippolytus.[6])

St. Paul also taught about sin, but in his teaching sin was different, as was redemption. Before we proceed with a very brief discussion of how St. Paul taught about sin, we need to stop and recognize that the way we think about sin is the result of 2,000 years of theological reflection on the New Testament. Doctoral dissertations have been and will be written about relationships between St. Paul's view of the nature of sin and the way later thinkers have viewed the nature of sin. Such studies lie far outside the scope of this book, other than to caution that whatever we, personally, see as the nature of sin may, or may not, be the way St. Paul looked at it.

Briefly, St. Paul included several lists of vices in his letters: Romans 1:29-31; I Corinthians 6:9-10; II Corinthians 12:20-21; Galatians 5:19-21, and a small list in Ephesians 4:31 (survey Ephesians 4 and 5 for more details). He also included a couple of lists of virtues: Galatians 5:22-23 and Philippians 4:8. Let's put the sins together (using NRSV wording) into some ad hoc groupings for convenience:

✧   General: Wickedness, evil, foolishness, investing in evil, silly talk.

✧   Blasphemy: Idolatry, sorcery, evil talk, craftiness, God-hating, faithlessness.

✧   Against society: Murder, disorder, robbery, thievery and stealing, rebellion toward parents, insolence, applauding others who sin.

✧   "Sins of the flesh:" Impurity and eagerness to be impure, licentiousness, sexual immorality, fornication, adultery, male prostitution, sodomy, drunkenness, carousing, obscene and vulgar talk.

✧Interpersonal: Gossip and slander, falsehood and deceit, quarreling and wrangling, malice, enmity, strife, dissension and factions, haughtiness, conceit, boasting, insensitivity, heartlessness, ruthlessness, selfishness, covetousness, greed, jealousy, envy, bitterness, reviling, anger and wrath.

  The pagan gods would not have recognized as sin any of those we have classified as "interpersonal." They would recognize some of the "sins of the flesh," depending on the god and the circumstances. Generally they would recognize "sins against society," and they would recognize "sins of blasphemy" if allowed to define the terms. The "interpersonal" category is huge! The religion of the pagan gods was missing an important point here.

  The Jews and St. Paul were not the only ones to recognize this deficit. The philosophers also recognized the need for systematic interpersonal responsibility. St. Paul was not concerned about a "system" of morality. He had no need to claim an exclusive morality, so he was satisfied with truth wherever it might come from. Most of his stated standards were Jewish, but some were from Stoic philosophy, such as Philippians 4:8: "Finally, beloved, whatever is true, whatever is honorable, whatever is just, whatever is pure, whatever is pleasing, whatever is commendable, if there is any excellence and if there is anything worthy of praise, think about these things."[7]

  Theologian Hans Küng makes the point that from the standpoint of Christian theology, the crucial consideration is not the source of St. Paul's teaching, but it is how a believer sees the teaching in relation to Christ.[8] This would be a crucial distinction for those in the Corinthian congregation who were well educated, but for those who were coming from the culture of pagan gods and goddesses, the inclusion of interpersonal responsibility as a mandate from God Almighty would have been wonderful good news.

---

1 Euripides, p. 349.

2 Euripides, p.358.

3 Euripides, p. 287.

4 Euripides, p. 292. Approx. lines 120-130.

5 Euripides, p. 361 Approx. lines 335-345.

6 Ovid, 1893A, pp. 29-41.

7 Küng, pp. 543-544.

8 Küng, pp. 543-544.

Common Meals and the Lord's Supper

Everywhere in the United States congregations gather from time to time to share a meal. Each family brings some food, and the food is set out on a large table so that each person who attends can eat some of all the food that has been brought. This common meal has many names: "pot-luck," "carry-in," "covered dish," etc., and people in various parts of the country claim that no one else does it "quite like" they do, but in fact, these meals are a universal aspect of church and community life throughout the U.S.

When we read I Corinthians 11:17-34, we sense that the Corinthian congregation also had pot-luck suppers, but that people weren't sharing as they should. Perhaps it was because of this that a ceremony was invented, which we call "Eucharist," or "Communion" or the "Lord's Supper." The ceremony takes the place of the common meal, making it impossible for participants to violate the unity of the community. Perhaps the ceremony existed earlier. St. Paul isn't clear about the ceremony, but he is clear about what was happening in the Corinthian congregation: "When you come together it is not really to eat the Lord's Supper. . . . In this matter I do not commend you!" (I Cor. 11:20, 22)

Certainly everyone would understand St. Paul's complaint. Hospitality is cross-cultural, and everyone recognizes inhospitable, unfriendly and contemptuous behavior.[1] Even so, we can benefit from a closer look at expectations related to the Passover, and expectations that ordinary Corinthians might have had.

First, it is clear that there was a strong tradition around the "Last Supper," the Passover meal Jesus shared with his disciples before he was crucified. That meal had made an indelible impression on those who attended, and they had told "everyone" about it. St. Paul had received and passed on this teaching, which he, as a Jew, understood very well.

The Passover meal is called "Seder," which means "order" (as in "order of service" or "order of worship").[2] There is a sequence in which things are to be done, and even though the precise procedure for the Seder may have changed a bit over the centuries, the Passover, whether modern or ancient, is a strict order of worship that requires participation. With this in mind, we can understand St. Paul's immediate outrage when he heard that some in the Corinthian congregation were eating, drinking, and even getting drunk, while others had not even arrived. To begin the celebration when some participants have not yet arrived violates the essential spirit of the Seder.

Today one can attend church services in which some people will arrive late, and occasionally some people will leave prior to the final benediction, but the service "works" in spite of the coming and going. In such services the congregation members are essentially passive. Certainly they participate in prayers and hymns, but they are more passive than not. That's why they can "come and go." In the Seder, everyone is involved in every portion of the service. They are not free to "come and go."

Of course, some members of the Corinthian congregation did not have a Jewish heritage, and might not be expected to appreciate the essential communal aspect of the seder. Was St. Paul's outrage against these people misplaced? Klinghardt has studied the descriptions of community meals in ancient Greek and Roman literature and concluded that *all* common meals shared a similar structure. Let's look at the Seder compared with the ancient secular meal (p. 220).

The "secular" column is a "stripped down" sequence. Each club or society would have its own ritual, but in all cases, the ritual fits this general pattern.[5] Klinghardt concludes that the difference in structure between pagan common meals and Jewish or early Christian common meals was simply the kind of religious expressions that were used. Both pagan and Jewish-Christian meals had a structure, and the structure was remarkably similar in both of them. Thus, we can conclude that the pagan converts in the Corinthian congregation should have been aware of the need to celebrate with everyone present and participating.

There is more.

Klinghardt also looked at the purpose of the ancient common meals, and found other points of similarity between pagan celebrations and Jewish or early Christian celebrations. Most important, all common meals reflected the ideal of "community" or koinonia. Related to "community" is "equality" (Greek, *isotes*). Equality was another ideal reflected

Seder	Secular
(1) Kiddush prayer. (2) Drinking the first cup of wine. (3) Tasting the vegetable dipped in salt water. (4) Breaking of unleavened bread. (5) Telling the Passover story. (6) Prayer and drinking the second cup of wine.	An appetizer and wine. (Relates to 1-6.)
(7) Ritual washing of hands. (8) Blessing the unleavened bread and distributing it. (9) Eating bitter herbs. (10) Bitter herb sandwich. (11) The regular meal. (12) Eat a bit of unleavened bread.[3]	A meal in several courses without wine. (Relates to 7-12.)
(13) Blessing and drinking third cup of wine. (14) Hallel Psalms and drinking fourth cup.	A religious ceremony involving singing one or more prayers
(15) Declaration that the meal is finished.[4]	Drinking and Entertainment

in these meals, even though it was not easy to achieve. In the quest to express equality, sometimes the wealthy and important served the slaves.[6] Meals were also supposed to reflect "good order," "quietness," and "peace." These qualities were sometimes difficult to sustain during the drinking parties that followed the meal, but pagan societies had rules, including fines for violations, to enforce the "good order."[7]

Now we have a "rounded" view of the reason for St. Paul's outrage. First, the sacred order of the Passover was violated. Second, even pagans were accustomed to order in common meals. Third, those who violated the order by eating and drinking out of turn had broken the peace. They were denying the unity of the congregation. This was one more symptom of the basic issue of disunity that prompted St. Paul to write the letter in the first place.

William Orr and James Walther examine the background of St. Paul's complaint in I Cor 11, and conclude that he is saying that those who violated the order of the meal and broken the peace, had actually done damage to the body of Christ. Orr and Walther think that when St. Paul quoted Jesus as saying "This is my body" after breaking the bread, St. Paul's idea was that the "this" to which Jesus referred was not the bread, but the entire order of service. Their reasoning is that meals were often referred to as "bread" (and we still speak of eating as "breaking bread.") St. Paul considered the Corinthian congregation to be modeled after the community of disciples celebrating the Passover. Both groups were the mutually dependent "body of Christ." When anyone violated the order of service, they were damaging the "body."[8]

---

1 Unless some members of the congregation were enamored of "Cynic" teaching—see the essay "A Character of Legend."

2 Donin, p. 229.

3 This is called the "*afikomen,*" and is sometimes thought of as a way to keep the attention of the children, as they hide it from the elders, or sometimes thought of as a dessert. Daube suggested that in ancient times this portion of bread symbolized the messiah, and that when Jesus said, "this is my body," he was referring to the *afikomen* and making a messianic claim. (See Carmichael in the bibliography.) See Orr and Walther for another interpretation.

4 Donin, pp. 233-236.

5 Klinghardt.

6 Klinghardt cites ancient writings of Theopompus of Chios, Strabo, Testament of Hiob, Philo, Lucian, and Plutarch, as well as descriptions of the Last Supper in the Gospels of Luke and John, when Jesus washed the feet of the disciples.

7 See the essay, "Sacramental Drunkenness."

8 Orr and Walther, pp. 272-273.

Speaking in Tongues

St. Paul felt that "speaking in tongues" was important enough that the topic deserved three chapters, out of sixteen in I Corinthians. So, what can we say about this from the perspective of life in Roman Corinth? Not much.

Is the experience in Corinth the same as the experience of the first apostles at Pentecost (Acts 2)? We don't know? Is the experience in Corinth the same as modern Pentecostalism? Although some will say a strong, "Yes!" to this, we really don't know. In the second century, the followers of Montanus spoke in tongues and Tertullian defended it. Was this second century experience the same as the experience in Corinth? We don't know.

Robertson and Plummer summarize the difficulty well, and even though they wrote more than 100 years ago, their conclusion is still valid:

The difficulty of this section lies in our ignorance of the condition of things to which it refers. The phenomena which are described, or
sometimes only alluded to, were to a large extent abnormal and transitory. They were not
part of the regular development of the Christian
Church. Even in Chrysostom's time there was
so much ignorance about them as to cause per-
plexity. He remarks that the whole of the passage is very obscure, because of our defective
information respecting facts, which took place
then, but take place no longer.[1]

Possibly the gift of "speaking in tongues" is purely a gift of
the Holy Spirit, with no cultural background, and if this is the
case, so be it. However, usually the Spirit of God is manifested
in ways that are in some sense intelligible in relation to the culture where the manifestation occurs. If God's Spirit were rou-
tinely manifested in ways totally independent of human culture,
theological thought would be impossible.

There is a broad consensus among scholars that Corinthians
would have understood "speaking in tongues" in relation to the
prophecies of the oracle at the Temple of Apollo in Delphi. To
travel from Corinth to Delphi was a relatively easy trip, and
everyone knew something about the oracles. Against the consensus, Forbes argues strongly, using Classical, Hellenistic, and
Roman writings, that Apollo's pronouncements at Delphi were
in Greek, not glossolalia, and that St. Paul did not describe the
glossolaia in the Corinthian congregation in Delphic terms.
Forbes makes a thorough review of modern scholarly writing
on Corinthian glossolia and rebuts those who claim that it was
influenced by Delphi.[2]

It has also been speculated that the Corinthian experience was somehow a reflection of the ecstatic celebrations in the cult of Dionysus.

It is far beyond the scope of this essay to examine or pass judgment on these scholarly debates, so we must simply say that we don't know. It is certainly possible that those claiming the gift of speaking in tongues were not directly influenced by Delphi or Dionysus, but that the cultural atmosphere that gave rise to the intoxicated cryptic sayings at Delphi and the wild drunken dances of Dionysus also gave opportunity for those who wanted to set themselves apart from others in the Corinthian congregation to claim a special gift of tongues. What we do know was well stated by Robertson and Plummer:

> All kinds of languages met at commercial Corinth with its harbours on two seas, and difference of language was a frequent barrier to common action. Moreover, it was well known how exasperating it could be for two intelligent persons to be unintelligible to one another. Yet the Corinthians were introducing these barriers and provocations into Christian worship, and all for the sake of display![3]

---

[1] Robertson and Plummer, p. 257.

[2] Forbes, 1986 and 1995.

[3] Robertson and Plummer, pp. 310-311.

A mirror cover on display in the Corinth museum.

SHORT HAIR, LONG HAIR, AND HEAD COVERINGS

First, a simple fact. The men in Corinth wore short hair. The women wore long hair, and did not wear it loose. Head coverings were common for pagan prayer. We know these things from the statues and paintings the Corinthians left behind.[1] The most notable exception to the standards is the god, Dionysus, who wore his hair long. (Images that show him as a young god-like a man in his 20s-show him with long hair. Images that show him as an old god-maybe in his 60s-show him with a standard male hair style.)

When we get a portrait made, we usually dress "formally," but we do not dress in an overcoat or other outdoor wear. This was probably true in the ancient world as well, so the portraits and statues don't show women veiled, but in ancient Greece and Rome, a woman walking in the streets would have worn a veil. An unveiled woman with loose hair would have been a "loose woman."

The playwright Euripides took advantage of this fact in order to let the audience know about the state of a character's mind. In *Hippolytus*, when we first see the female lead, Phaedra, she is having a fit of madness, sometimes attempting to appear "proper," and, in the same scene, shifting to show her sexual frustration.[2] When she is clear-headed and "proper," she is veiled, but when she lapses into madness, she throws the veil off and displays her loose hair. The stage business with the veil augments the words she speaks.

Euripides lived several hundred years before St. Paul, but the customs seem to have been very stable because the idea that "good" women did not wear their hair loose was assumed a century after St. Paul in the apocryphal Christian book, *The Shepherd of Hermas*. The second half of this book consists of a series of dreams or visions, and the Shepherd sees faithful Christians being led astray by "twelve women, very beautiful to look at, clothed in black, girded, and their shoulders bare, and their hair loose." These loose-haired women were named Unbelief, Impurity, Disobedience, Deceit, Grief, Wickedness, Licentiousness, Bitterness, Lying, Foolishness, Evil-speaking, and Hate.[3]

Second, a straightforward bit of background: St. Paul, speaking as an interpreter of Jewish law, was advising the Corinthian congregation to observe Jewish law. Jewish law required a woman to keep her head covered unless she was in the privacy of her own home. Otherwise she was admitting to being "loose." Derrett refers us to the Mishna for an explanation as to why women were required to cover their heads in public: "A woman's hair is a sexual incitement."[4] Therefore, the woman's husband, who has a right (as his wife's "head") to expect her to behave modestly, has a right to expect her to cover her head.

Apparently the problem had to do with women who reasoned that because everyone is equal in Christ, they didn't need to cover their heads in worship. (see Gal. 3:28) Furthermore, by not covering their heads, they were differentiating themselves from the other women of Corinth, especially the pagan women. (Of course, they were not differentiating themselves from the "loose" pagan women!)

Freedom without wisdom is futile, and St. Paul saw a need to set these women straight. Of course, if they didn't have hair, then there would be no sexual incitement, so no need for a head cover.

If we are looking no further than to understand the essence of St. Paul's instructions in I Cor. 11:2-16, then we have enough information. But if we want to understand the culture in which the Corinthian congregation functioned, there is more to be said.

Why was long hair a sexual incitement? Of course every culture has an understanding of what constitutes "sexual incitement." For example, consider the title song from the 1938 Broadway musical, "Anything Goes." The first line of the song says, "In olden days a glimpse of stocking was looked on as something shocking . . ." In other words, when women wore long skirts, a female ankle was enough to turn men's heads. In contrast, in the practically undressed society of today, sometimes a bit of clothing will turn men's heads. In any case, in every society there is something that women can do with their hair, their eyes, their clothing, their bodies, or whatever, to manufacture "sexual incitement."

Today, certain hair styles may turn heads, but in general "hair" is not something men pay attention to. Why was hair such a big concern in the ancient world?

The answer takes us into an unexpected realm that demonstrates how difficult it is for us to really understand an ancient culture. Troy W. Martin has published a thoroughly scholarly, but very frank (and maybe somewhat "raw") article in which he explains popular understandings of human anatomy in St. Paul's world.[5] A person would anticipate that, because of the anatomical studies conducted by Galen and his followers, there would be a pretty good understanding of basic human anatomy in the Roman world. After all, Galen and his followers had dissected many corpses in their effort to understand human sickness. Furthermore, most people (especially in Corinth) had a chance to see fighters slaughter one another in gladiatorial combat.

Even so, most people did not really understand anatomy, and they especially did not understand reproductive anatomy. Martin's article presents persuasive evidence that most people in St. Paul's time considered human hair to be an integral part of reproductive anatomy. Without going into (what for this publication would be) inappropriate detail, suffice it to say that a female display of long hair would be equivalent to displaying genitilia, because hair was considered to be a real part of the reproductive system. Hair was not just a symbol for sexual identity, hair actually was sexual identity. "Why?" you may ask. "How was hair believed to be part of the reproductive system?" Martin presents the answers to these questions in detail, and the answers sound grotesque to our ears.

When we first read the evidence that Martin provides, our first reaction is likely to be, "This is silly." It takes a while to understand that Martin is reporting about the actual understanding that common people had, and that they really believed that hair was a part of the genital system. The belief was common among Greeks and Jews, and St. Paul likely believed it as well. Much of what St. Paul and other biblical writers say has to do with universals of the human condition, and it is these parts of the Bible that we find most useful in guiding our daily lives. Beyond this, archeology, anthropology, philology and related sciences have helped us understand the people for whom the Bible was originally written, but we must have the humility to admit that there will always be parts of the ancient culture that are simply beyond our comprehension. Whenever we say, "The Corinthians believed . . ." or "The Corinthians knew . . ." or "The Corinthians acted as if . . ." we must be prepared to admit that we were mistaken.

---

1 Thompson.

2 Euripides, pp. 295-303. The standard line notation is from around 290 to around 380. Some translations do not include stage notations, but Gilbert Murray's translation makes the putting on and taking off of the veil very clear.

3 *Shepherd of Hermas*, pp. 241-261 (sim. IX ix-xv).

4 Derrett, fn. 5.

5 Martin.

The Erastus Monument

ERASTVS • PRO • AED
S • P • STRAVIT

INDIVIDUALS OF NOTE

We don't know the people in the Corinthian congregation, but we certainly wish we did. First Corinthians is so personal that we would really like to know the personalities in that congregation. Consequently, many readers have imagined personalities for the people addressed by St. Paul, and our imaginations are enriched by the fact that we have some names.

Phoebe was evidently not in Corinth, but in the town at the port of Chenchreae. Was she perhaps one of the early members of the Corinthian congregation who saw a need for the Gospel to be preached in the port, so close to the city, yet so far away? Cenchreae belonged to Posidon, the god of the sea, but was being taken over by the oriental upstart, Isis. Neither offered the positive hope that came from following Christ. Phoebe was a woman. Could she start a congregation? Would St. Paul approve? In light of I Timothy 2:11-12, one might wonder, but St. Paul certainly did approve, and apparently he also trusted her to deliver his important letter to the Romans! (Rom. 16:1-2). Don't we wish we knew more!

St. Luke tells us that the house church was established in the residence of Titus Justus (Acts 18:7), and St. Paul speaks of Gaius as host to the church (Rom. 16:23 and I Cor. 1:14). Edgar Goodspeed suggested that these are the same person: Gaius Titus Justus would be his full Roman name.[1] Of course we don't know, but this makes sense. What else can we say about him? Probably he was wealthy, otherwise he would not have been able to host the congregation. Probably he brought his family and some slaves into the congregation. St. Paul probably used the resources of the household when he wrote to the congregation at Rome, and since Tertius was the secretary who transcribed the letter (Romans 16:22), he might have been a slave of Gaius Titus Justus. Probably Gaius had been a worshipper in the synagogue, but with a Roman name he may not have been Jewish. Quite possibly he was one of the "God fearers." Which side was he on in the disputes? St. Paul seems to like him, so maybe he was a wise leader who did not take part in the quarreling. That's all we can say, and it is mostly speculation.

Stephanus is mentioned more often than any of the others. He was the first convert in Corinth (I Cor. 16:15), St. Paul baptized him and his household (I Cor. 1:16), and he led the delegation which came to Ephesus to ask for guidance (I Cor. 16:17). What else can we say? If he was the first convert, it is likely that he worshipped in the synagogue where he first met St. Paul. However, our imaginations can dream up a story saying that Priscilla and Aquila had met him before St. Paul arrived, and that they had told him about the new messiah, Jesus.

If he was free to travel, we would think that he was wealthy. Who did he represent when he brought his questions? Some of the questions had come from "Chloe's people."

(I Cor. 1:11) Did Stephanus and his companions bring the letter from Chloe, or had Chloe's letter been delivered another way, so that Stephanus represented a different party? We simply don't know.

What about Chloe? Theissen speculates that "Chloe's people" were slaves or low class workers.[2] He notes that if they had constituted a family, they would have been grouped under the father's name (even if he were dead). Since the group was represented by a woman, they were likely low class (even if Chloe, herself, might have been wealthy).[3] Theissen points out that St. Paul takes the side of the lower class members of the congregation (I Cor. 1:12ff and 11:17-34).

Then there is Erastus, about whom there has been more speculation than about any of the other people in the congregation. St. Paul calls him "the city treasurer" (RSV) or "manager" (Rom. 16:23), and in 1929 archeologists in Corinth discovered a large inscription[4] that apparently says, "Erastus for his *aedileship* laid [the pavement] at his own expense." *Aediles* were elected officials who held office for one year, and were responsible for the maintenance of public streets and buildings, managed public money, and served as judges. In return for the honor of holding public office, they were expected to pay for at least some of the maintenance out of their own pockets. Monuments by *aediles* were fairly common in the Roman Empire.[5]

What can we say about the Erastus of Romans 16:23? Cadbury examined the evidence from around the Roman Empire, and concluded that the office of "treasurer" or "manager" in Roman Corinth would have been held by a well educated slave (who might have been wealthy).[6] In contrast, an *aedile* held a different office and would have been a wealthy freedman. In that case, Erastus of the inscription would be a different person from St. Paul's friend. Cadbury admits that in our imagination we might think of Erastus as a slave who had become wealthy, and who held the office of "treasurer," was manumitted during the time of his office, was elected as an *aedile*, and provided the pavement.[7] In Cadbury's opinion, this is extremely unlikely, but possible.[8] Is that the end of it?

In 1989, Gill reviewed the scholarly comments on this issue since Cadbury's 1931 article, and there had been no solid advances.

In 2009, Goodrich examined the issue again in light of a newly discovered inscription from the Achaean colony of Patras, and argued that St. Paul's friend, Erastus served as *quaestor*, a high-ranking municipal position exclusively occupied by the economic elite, not as an *aedile*.[9] Once again, everything is speculative.

The matter of Erastus is made more complicated by the fact that someone named Erastus is mentioned three times in the New Testament: Romans 16:23; II Timothy 4:20; and Acts 19:21. Are these the same person? Are they two different people? Are they three people? We simply don't know, and again are left to our imaginations.

Several other people are mentioned in relation to the congregation at Corinth, but we don't even have enough information about them to stir our imaginations. Maybe this is good. If we knew these people too well, we might easily pass by St. Paul's hard teachings in his letters with the assumption that they apply only to Phoebe, Gaius Titus Justus, Stephanus, Chloe, or Erastus. Because we don't really know who these people are, we are able to see the teachings as applicable to us today as well as to the ancient congregation.

1 Goodspeed, pp. 382-383.

2 Theissen, pp. 93-95.

3 Theissen, p. 57.

4 Cadbury.

5 Gill, p. 295.

6 Cadbury, pp. 51-52.

7 Cadbury, p. 56.

8 Cadbury's best known comment is in the last paragraph of his detailed and complicated article, "The upshot of our discussion is that the identification of the Erastus of the inscription with a New Testament character is improbable if not impossible," although he had admitted the possibility earler, p. 58.

9 Goodrich.

The Temple of Octavia recognized the family of Emperor Augustus as worthy of worship. It was under construction when St. Paul was in Corinth.

A NEW VIEW OF LOVE

If a person knows only one word of Greek, it is *agape*.
How should we translate this word? When St. Jerome translated
the New Testament into Latin, he chose the word, *caritas*,
which the King James translators accepted as "charity." The
Latin *caritas* is probably derived from the Greek word *charis*,
which was seen as something delightful which leads to joy, and
which became, in the New Testament, the word for the grace of
God.

According to Constantelos, "In ancient Greek society, charity was synonymous with love (*agape, philanthropia, eleos*,
and *philoxenia*) and it was manifested through benevolent
deeds on behalf of those in need."[1] This suggests that St.
Jerome and the King James translators were not "out of
bounds" in their translation, although *charis* (grace) was a special word for St. Paul, so that one may wonder about translating
agape in terms of *charis*.[2]

In the past century, everyone who has published an English version of the New Testament has translated agape as "love." This is probably more accurate than "charity," depending on what the word "love" means.

As the saying goes, "The Greeks had a word for it." While English struggles with the concept of "love," using one word for many purposes, the ancient Greeks had three primary words that are translated into English by the one word, "love."

"*Eros*" was perhaps the primary word, certainly used for the concept we call "erotic," but also used for highly abstract and spiritualized concepts. In other words, it was an "all purpose" word for "love," similar to the way that the word "love" serves many purposes in English.[3] The patristic theologian Origin was probably the first scholar to recognize that "eros" is not used in the New Testament. It is really not easy for us to explain why the New Testament authors avoided the word.[4]

"*Philia*" was used for love of gods and friends from whom we expected something in return[5], but it was also used to describe Jesus' relationship with his disciples, not really a relationship of reciprocity (John 16:27; 21:15-17. See also Titus 3:15 with respect to St. Paul). Arndt and Gingrich define the word as "have affection for."[6]

"*Agape*" was, for the ancient Greeks, a "colorless" word, often used as a variation for one of the other two words.[7] How, then, did *agape* become the preferred New Testament word for "love?" The New Testament use came from the Greek translation of the Old Testament, the Septuagint. Before the New Testament, *agape* was a "special" word only in the Septuagint and in the writings of people (like Philo) who had been educated in the Septuagint, but even in the Septuagint it was not as "special" as it became in the New Testament.

Some have tried to make a case that St. Paul used this word because it had been used in reference to the goddess Isis, queen of one of the "mystery religions," but Griffiths, who has studied the issue, says, "As for the scope of meaning, the quality of *agape* in Isis herself, if we apply it to the various facets of her affection, clearly includes sexual love, for she is said to ordain the physical union of men and women. Here there is a sharp contrast to Christian usage. Other facets are certainly comparable with those of the Christian concept, particularly her benevolence and saving power."[8] So even though there exists a passing reference to Isis as the goddess of *agape*, St. Paul was not making any kind of allusion to Isis in his writing. He was a Greek speaking Jew who was employing the vocabulary of the Septuagint.

St. Paul, then, took the word, *agape*, from the Septuagint, but the Septuagint doesn't distinguish as clearly among the three words for love as St. Paul does. It was out of his concern over the dispute in the Corinthian congregation about speaking in tongues that he composed the poem we have as I Corinthians 13, "Though I speak in the tongues of men and angels, but have not *agape* . . ." Although the word is used throughout the New Testament, the literary force of this poem, presented to the congregation at Corinth, elevated the word so that it became unavoidably related to a specific concept.

We return to the question of what *agape* "means" in the New Testament. Today, Christians are unavoidably influenced as to the Christian meaning of "agape" by the exhaustive and powerful theological study by Anders Nygren, *Agape and Eros*,[9] one of the most influential works of theological scholarship in the 20th Century.

It is not the purpose of this book, with its intentionally brief essays, to pass judgment on complex theological issues. Nygren's work has been commented on almost endlessly, but here we mention it simply to say that when we read the great poem called I Corinthians 13, we should understand that St. Paul was taking a "colorless" word and defining it for new followers of Jesus in terms of belief and action. Once he had defined it, he presented it to this disputatious congregation as the most basic of Christian gifts (*chairsmata*): ". . . but the greatest of these is love." How startling would this have been for these people, each of whom was loudly proclaiming that their personal gift was the greatest?

The later theological discussions about *agape* are good for us, helping us sort out how we should live as followers of Jesus in our time, but if we want to enter into the minds of the ancient Corinthians (as much as that is possible), we need to clear out our preconceptions about the proper translation of *agape*, and listen to the way in which St. Paul was giving them a truly new word.

---

1 Constantelos, p. 223.

2 See Conzelmann.

3 Stauffer, p. 7.

4 Rist, p. 236.

5 Stauffer, p. 7

6 Arndt and Gingrich, p. 866.

[7] Stauffer, p. 7.

[8] Griffiths, p. 141.

[9] Nygren.

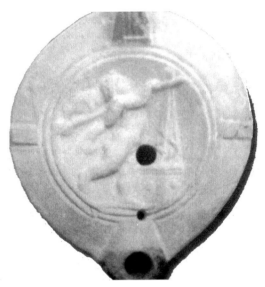

Clay oil lamp with a picture of Eros.
Such lamps, with a wide variety of pictures, were manufactured by the thousands. This one is on display in the
Corinth museum.

THE HERESY OF SELF-CENTEREDNESS

If there is a theme for the Corinthian letters, it is "arrogance," or being "puffed up," as the KJV so aptly says. St. Paul speaks about the general concept of "arrogance" before he starts to comment about specific sinful actions. ". . . some of you, thinking that I am not coming to you, have become arrogant. But I will come to you soon, if the Lord wills, and I will find out not the talk of these arrogant people but their power. For the kingdom of God depends not on talk but on power." (I Cor. 4:18-20.)

Their arrogance is reflected in several behaviors, and these behaviors seem to come from a slogan that the offenders claim is a summary of St. Paul's teaching: "All things are lawful for me." (I Cor. 6:12.)

For almost 2,000 years, students of St. Paul's writings have had trouble with this saying, because when he wrote his letters, quotation marks had not yet been invented. The crucial question is, when St. Paul says, "All things are lawful for me," is he voicing his own understanding of the teaching of Jesus, or is he quoting a slogan current in the Corinthian congregation? The current consensus of New Testament scholars is that this is a Corinthian slogan.[1] St. Paul does not agree that we should consider all things to be acceptable under the law of God.

Among others, John Calvin, the reformer, commented, "It is probable that the Corinthians even up to that time retained much of their former licentiousness, and had still a savor of the morals of their city. . . . These words, 'All things are lawful for me,' must be understood as spoken in the name of the Corinthians, . . . as though he had said, I am aware of the reply which you are accustomed to make, when desirous to avoid reproof for outward vices. You pretend that all things are lawful for you, without any reserve or limitation."[2]

Where did the slogan come from? A person who didn't listen closely to St. Paul's carefully formed teaching could come away with the notion that God doesn't care about our behavior. After all, didn't he say that circumcision was irrelevant to salvation? Didn't he say that it is not absolutely wrong to eat food offered to idols?

More important is that this slogan resonated with popular culture. Diogenes the Cynic, whose grave was a prominent landmark in Corinth, taught that everyone should be free to do anything they wanted to do.[3] The stories about his "freedom," even when he was a slave, became part of his legend. Likewise, the Stoic philosophical teachers proclaimed this sort of "freedom." A generation later, Gnosticism, a perversion of Christianity, would teach the same thing, and even though Gnosticism was not well developed in St. Paul's day, its seeds were in the culture.[4] Those who had studied philosophy might have been the first to proclaim this slogan as "truth," but it wouldn't have taken long for everyone to adopt such a self-centered view of the new faith.

The notion of "freedom" is inherently paradoxical. Every time one person exercises "freedom," that person inevitably limits the "freedom" of someone else. When I enter the door first, no one else can enter first. On a larger scale, if I exercise my "freedom" to drive without a seat belt and get hurt in a wreck, the hospital resources I use cannot be used by anyone else. St. Paul points out that when I use my "freedom" to hire someone to be my sexual partner, I lose certain freedoms in relation to my spouse and in relation to God. (I Cor. 6:16-17.)

In addition to this social problem, there is an individual problem. Often a person thinks they are exercising "freedom," when they are actually restricting their greater freedom. We may think that we are exercising "freedom" when we smoke, drink, or gamble, but to the degree that we become addicted to these behaviors, we restrict the "freedom" we thought we had.

St. Paul understood these inherent problems in the notion of "freedom," and taught carefully, saying such things as, "'All things are lawful for me', but I will not be dominated by anything." (I Cor. 6:12b), and the highly nuanced phrase, "I am not free from God's law but am under Christ's law." (I Cor. 9:21b). Fee points to I Cor 3:21-23 and 10:23, and offers this ethical summary: "Truly Christian conduct is not predicated on whether I have the right to do something, but whether my conduct is helpful to those about me."[5] This returns us to the notion of "love" as the controlling ethical concept: "love is not envious or boastful or arrogant or rude." (I Cor. 13:4.)

As we have seen, the Corinthian congregation was a mixture of people. The "good news" that St. Paul taught was for each of the groups in the congregation, and as we finish this collection of essays, we can summarize the two-pronged message that St. Paul brought to Corinth. Some people followed the flesh, and some were concerned with the soul, and all were misguided. Following the flesh leads to interpersonal strife and licentiousness, while following the soul leads to self-centered arrogance and licentiousness. People most concerned with the "flesh" are probably those who have been attracted to the mystery religions, while those most concerned with the soul are probably those who have been attracted to the philosophers. In either case, they have become self-centered.

St. Paul called on everyone to serve not the flesh and not the soul, but the "body." The "body" is the "Body of Christ." It is the congregation. It is all those who might turn to the congregation. It is everyone for whom Jesus lived, taught, died, and was raised.

---

[1] Thiselton, p. 461, fn. 192, presents a summary of the many scholars who see it as a Corinthian slogan, and the very few scholars who disagree and say that this phrase expresses St. Paul's opinion. Interestingly, the classic commentary by Robertson and Plummer, which we have referenced in some of these essays, holds the minority opinion.

[2] Calvin, John (tr. John King). *Calvin's Commentary on I Corinthians*, 1847.

[3] See the essay, "A Character of Legend." Pausanias found the grave of Diogenes to be a Corinthian monument worth visiting. Pausanias II.4, p. 257.

[4] See the essay, "How Good is God?" See also Fee, p. 251, fn.

[5] Fee, p. 251.

Who will you serve?

Body   Soul
(Aphrodite)   (Platonism)
(Isis)   (Stoicism)
(Dionysus)   (Gnosticism)

* * * * * * * * * * * * * * * * * *

Serve   Serve
Body   Soul

Lack of self   Personal
discipline   arrogance

* * * * * * * * * * * * * * * * *

Third Option

Serve Others
Through Christ

(ex: II Cor. 11:16-33, St. Paul's personal
testimony, and I Cor. 13, love one another.)

An ancient
anchor.

CHRONOLOGY

776 First Olympic Games

484 Euripides born at Salamis

Classical Period: 480 BCE to 323 BCE

469 Socrates born

455 Euripides' first play produced

430 Plato born

438 Pindar dies

411 Aristophanes' *Thesmophoriazusae*

406 Bacchae

399 Socrates dies

386 Plato founds Academy

384 Aristotle born

377 Hippocrates of Cos dies

347 Plato dies

Hellenistic Period: 323 BCE to 31 BCE

323 Diogenes the Cynic and Alexander the Great both die.

322 Aristotle dies

275 Septuagint Bible

146 Corinth destroyed by General Mummius

100 Julius Caesar born

44 Corinth reestablished as a Roman Colony

44 Julius Caesar murdered

Early Roman Period: 31 BCE to 250 CE

31 Battle of Actium. Octavius defeats Antony and Cleopatra.

29 Strabo visits Corinth

27 Augustus becomes emperor

19 Virgil's Aeneid

27 BCE-14 CE Augustus (Octavian)

14 – 37 Tiberius

17 Ovid dies

Resurrection of Jesus

31 Conversion of St. Paul

39 Philo in Rome

37 – 41 Caligula

48 – 49 Council of Jerusalem

41 – 54 Claudius

50—51 St. Paul in Corinth

54 – 68 Nero

100 Juvenal at his height

61 – 112 Pliny the Younger, letter writer

64 Burning of Rome

70 Destruction of Jerusalem by Titus

79 Eruption of Vesuvius

98 – 117 Emperor Trajan

c. 125 Plutarch dies.

120-150 "Shepherd of Hermas" written

131 Galen the physician born

162 Galen comes to Rome

150 – 212 Clement of Alexandria

160 – 225 Tertullian

161 – 180 Marcus Aurelius

BIBLIOGRAPHY

Amelung, W. "Notes on Representations of Socrates and of Diogenes and Other Cynics," *American Journal of Archaeology,* v. 31, no. 3 (Jul-Sep 1927), pp. 281-296.

Apuleius (tr. by Jack Lindsay). *The Golden Ass.* Bloomington: Indiana University Press, 1960.

Aristophenes, (tr. Henry Fielding and William Young). *Plutus, the God of Riches.* No publisher indicated. No date.

Aristophenes (tr. Benjamin Bickley Rogers). *The Thesmophoriazusae of Aristophanes.* London: George Bell & Sons, 1904.

Aristotle (tr. W. D. Ross). "Metaphysics" in *Aristotle, Vol. I* (Great Books of the Western World, Vol. 8). Encyclopaedia Britannica, 1952.

Arndt, William F. and F. Wilbur Gingrich. *A Greek-English Lexicon of the New Testament and Other Early Christian Literature.* University of Chicago Press, 1957.

Barclay, William. *The Letters to the Corinthians,* Rev. Ed. Philadelphia: Westminster, 1956.

Barth, Markus. *Ephesians: Introduction, Translation, and Commentary on Chapters 1-3* (The Anchor Bible). Garden City, NY: Doubleday & Co., Inc., 1974.

Bonner, Campbell, "A Dionysiac Miracle at Corinth," *American Journal of Archaeology,* v. 33, no. 3 (1929), pp. 368-375.

Bookidis, Nancy and Ronald S. Stroud. *Demeter and Persephone in Ancient Corinth.* Princeton, N.J.: American School of Classical Studies at Athens, 1987, p. 301.

Bornkamm, G., "mysterion," in Bromiley, Geoffrey W., *Theological Dictionary of the New Testament . . . Abridged in One Volume.* Eerdmans, 1985, pp. 615-619.

Bowes, Kim, "Early Christian Archaeology: A State of the Field," *Religion Compass,* v. 2, no. 4, 2008, pp. 575-61. www.arts.cornell.edu/classics/faculty/ KBowes_files/early christian archaeology religion compass.pdf

Broneer, Oscar. "Corinth: Center of St. Paul's Missionary Work in Greece," *The Biblical Archeologist,* v. 14, no. 4 (Dec. 1951), pp. 78-96.

Budge, E. A. Wallis. *The Dwellers on the Nile: The Life, History, Religion and Literature of the Ancient Egyptians.* New York: Dover, 1977, reprint of the 1926 edition.

Budin, Stephanie L. "Sacred Prostitution in the First Person," in *Prostitutes and Courtesans in the Ancient World.* (ed. Christopher A. Faraone and Laura K. McClure.) University of Wisconsin Press, 2006, pp. 77-92.

Cadbury, Henry J. "Erastus of Corinth," *Journal of Biblical Literature,* v. 50, no. 2 (1931), pp. 42-58.

Capps, Edward, Jr. "Observations on the Painted Venatio of the Theatre at Corinth and on the Arrangements of the Arena," *Hesperia Supplements, Vol. 8, Commemorative Studies in Honor of Theodore Leslie Shear,* 1949, pp. 64-70 and 444-445.

Carmichael, Deborah Bleicher, "David Daube on the Eucharist and the Passover Seder," in Evans, Craig A. and Stanley E. Porter. *New Testament Backgrounds.* Sheffield Academic Press, 1997, pp. 89-108.

Classen, C. Joachim, "St Paul's Epistles and Ancient Greek and Roman Rhetoric," *Rhetorica*, v. X, no. 4 (1992), pp. 319-344.

Clement of Rome (tr. Kirsopp Lake). "The First Epistle of Clement to the Corinthians," in *The Apostolic Fathers, Vol I.* Cambridge, MA: Harvard University Press (Loeb Classical Library), 1912.

Cline, Maryanne Horowitz, "Aristotle and Women," *Journal of the History of Biology*, v. 9, no. 2, 1976, pp. 183-213.

Constantelos, Demetrios J. "Charity," in Eliade, Mircea. *The Encyclopedia of Religion*, Vol 3. New York: Macmillan, 1987, pp. 222-225.

Conzelmann, H., "cháris, charízomai, charitóô, acháristos," in Bromiley, Geoffrey W. *Theological Dictionary of the New Testament, Abridged in One Volume* (Kittel and Friedrich). William B. Eerdmans Publishing Company/ Paternoster Press, 1985, pp. 1301-1305.

Cook, R. M. "Archaic Greek Trade: Three Conjectures," *The Journal of Hellenic Studies*, v. 99 (1979), pp. 152-155.

Csapo, Eric, "Riding the Phallus for Dionysus: Iconology, Ritual, and Gender -Role De/Construction," *Phoenix*, v. 51, no. 3-4 (1997), pp. 253-295.

Davies, J. G. *The Origin and Development of Early Christian Church Architecture.* SCM Press, 1952.

DeMaris, Richard E., "Corinthian Religion and Baptism for the Dead (I Corinthians 15:29): Insights from Archaeology and Anthropology," *Journal of Biblical Literature*, v. 114, no. 4 (1995-A), pp. 661-682.

DeMaris, Richard E. "Demeter in Roman Corinth: Local Development in a Mediterranean Religion," *Numen*, v. 42, no. 2 (1995-B), pp. 105-117.

Derrett, J. Duncan M. "Religious Hair," *Man (New Series)*, v. 8, no. 1 (1973), pp. 100-103.

Dillon, John. *The Middle Platonists, 80 B.C. to A.D. 220.* Ithaca, NY: Cornell U. P., 1977.

Diogenes Laertius (tr by A. Robert Caponigri). *Lives of the Philosophers.* Chicago: Henry Regnery Co., 1969.

Donin, Hayim Halevy. *To Be a Jew: A Guide to Jewish Observance in Contemporary Life.* NY: Basic Books, 1972.

Dover, Kenneth James. *Greek Popular Morality in the Time of Plato and Aristotle.* Basil Blackwell, 1974, 1994.

Dumas, Alexandre (tr by Henry William Herbert). *Acte of Corinth, or, the Convert of Saint Paul: A Tale of Greece and Rome* (a novel). New York: Garrett & Co., 1852.

Edwards, H. J. "Commerce and Industry,"in Whibley, Leonard (ed). *A Companion to Greek Studies.* Cambridge: University Press, 1905, pp. 426 – 438.

Erman, Adolf (tr. A. S. Griffith). *A Handbook of Egyptian Religion.* London: Archibald Constable & Co., Ltd., 1907.

Euripides (Eliot, Charles W., ed. The Euripides dramas tr. Gilbert Murray.) *Nine Greek Dramas* (The Harvard Classics, Vol. 8). New York: P. F. Collier & Son, 1909.

Fee, Gordon D. *The First Epistle to the Corinthians.*(The New International Commentary on the New Testament). Eerdmans, 1987.

Ferguson, Everett. *Backgrounds of Early Christianity* (2nd ed.). Grand Rapids, MI: Eerdmans, 1993.

Forbes, Christopher, "Early Christian Inspired Speech and Hellenistic Popular Religion," *Novum Testamentum,* v. 28 (1986), pp. 257-270.

Forbes, Christopher. *Prophecy and Inspired Speech in Early Christianity and its Hellenistic Environment.* Tübingen: Mohr, 1995.

Fraser, P. M. "The ΔΙΟΛΚΟΣ of Alexandria," *The Journal of Egyptian Archaeology*, v. 47 (Dec. 1961), pp. 134-138.

Furley, William D. *Studies in the Use of Fire in Ancient Greek Religion.* NY: Arno Press, 1981.

Furnish, Victor Paul, *The Moral Teaching of Paul,* second edition. Abingdon Press, 1985. (Esp. ch III, pp. 52-82.)

Gaster, T. H. "Sacrifices and Offerings, OT," in Buttrick, G. A., et. al., (eds). *The Interpreter's Dictionary of the Bible.* Vol. 4. Abingdon Press, 1962, pp. 147-159.

Gebhard, Elizabeth R. and Matthew W. Dickie. *Corinth, The Centenary: 1896 -1996 (Corinth, Vol. 20).* American School of Classical Studies at Athens, 2003, pp. 261-278.

Gill, David W. J. "Erastus the Aedile," *Tyndale Bulletin,* v. 40, no. 2 (1989), 293-301.

Griffiths, J. Gwyn, "Isis and Agape" (Notes and Discussions), *Classical Philology,* v. 80, no. 2 (1985), pp. 139-141.

Golden, Mark. *Greek Sport and Social Status.* Austin: U. of Texas Press, 2008.

Goodrich, John K., "Erastus, Quaestor of Corinth: The Administrative Rank of ὁ οἰκονόμος τῆς πόλεως (Rom 16:23) in an Achaean Colony," *New Testament Studies,* v. 56 (2010), pp. 90-115.

Goodspeed, Edgar J., "Gaius Titus Justus," *Journal of Biblical Literature,* vol. 69, no. 4, (1950).

Grant, Frederick C. *Hellenistic Religions: The Age of Syncretism.* Indianapolis: Bobbs-Merrill (Library of Liberal Arts), 1953.

Grant, Michael. *The World of Rome.* New American Library: Mentor, 1960.

Greenhill, William A. "Galenus, Claudius" and "Hippocrates" in Smith, William, ed. *A Dictionary of Greek and Roman Biography and Mythology,* Vol II. London: John Murray, 1880, pp. 207-217, 482-489.

Grindheim, Sigurd, "Wisdom for the Perfect: Paul's Challenge to the Corinthian Church (I Corinthians 2:6-16)," *Journal of Biblical Literature,* v. 121, no. 4 (2002), pp. 689-709.

Haddad, Naif and Talal Akasheh, "Vitruvius and Ancient Theatres," Hashemite University, Zarqa 13115, Jordan, http://cultech.org/Vetruvius.pdf.

Harris, H. A. *Greek Athletes and Athletics.* Westport, CN: Greenwood Press, 1964.

Harris, H. A. *Greek Athletics and the Jews.* Cardiff: University of Wales Press, 1976.

Harrison, Jane. *Prolegomena to the Study of Greek Religion.* New York: Meridian Books, 1955, reprint of the 1922 edition.

Henrichs, Albert, "Between City and Country: Cultic Dimensions of Dionysus in Athens and Attica," *Cabinet of the Muses: Rosenmeyer Festschrift.* UC Berkeley: Department of Classics, UCB: http://www.escholarship.org/uc/item/5xt4952c, cf. p. 271. Cabinet of the Muses, ed. M. Griffith and D. J. Mastronarde, pp. 257-277, ©1990 Scholars Press, ©2005 Dept. of Classics, Univ. of California, Berkeley.

Heyob, Sharon Kelly. *The Cult of Isis Among Women in the Graeco-Roman World.* E. J. Brill, 1975.

Hill, Andrew E. "The Temple of Asclepius: An Alternative Source for Paul's Body Theology?" *Journal of Biblical Literature,* v. 99, no. 3 (Sep. 1980), pp. 437-439.

Hock, Ronald F. "Paul's Tentmaking and the Problem of His Social Class," *Journal of Biblical Literature,* v. 97. No. 4 (1978), pp. 555-564.

Hollenweger, Walter J. *Conflict in Corinth and Memoirs of an Old Man: Two Stories the Illuminate the Way the Bible Came to be Written.* Ramsey, NJ: Paulist Press, 1982.

Homer (tr. S. H. Butcher and A. Lang). *The Odyssey of Homer.* (The Harvard Classics, Vol. 22). New York: P. F. Collier & Son, 1909.

Hopkins, Clark. *The Christian Church at Dura-Europos. Vol. 1. The Christian Church.* Yale U. P., 1934.

Howe, George and G. A. Harper, *A Handbook of Classical Mythology.* London: George Allen and Unwin, 1931, Oracle Publising, 1996.

Imhoof-Blumer, F. and Percy Gardner. *A Numismatic Commentary on Pausanias.* Reprinted from the Journal of Hellenic Studies, 1885, 1886, 1887.

Jacobson, D. M. and M. P. Weitzman, "What Was Corinthian Bronze?" *American Journal of Archaeology,* v. 96, no. 2, (Apr. 1992), pp. 237-247.

Judge, E. A. "Cultural Conformity and Innovation in Paul: Some Clues from Contemporary Documents," (Tyndale Biblical Archaeology Lecture, 1983), *Tyndale Bulletin* 36 (1984) 3-24. http://98.131.162.170/tynbul/library/TynBull_1984_35_01_Judge_CulturalConformityPaul.pdf.

Juvenal (tr. Hubert Creekmore). *The Satires of Juvenal.* New American Library Mentor Book, 1963.

Juvanal (tr. William Gifford). *The Satires of Decimus Junius Juvenalis.* London: W. Bulmer and Co., 1802.

Kardulias, P. Nick. *From Classical to Byzantine: Social Evolution in Late Antiquity in the Fortress at Isthmia, Greece.* Archaeopress (British Archaeological Reports) #1412, 2005.

Klausner, Joseph. (tr. William F. Stinespring). *From Jesus to Paul.* NY: Macmillan, 1943.

Klinghardt, Matthias, "A Typology of the Community Meal (Draft Version)," paper presented at the Annual Meeting of the Society for Biblical Literature, 2003.

Kraemer, Ross, S. "Ecstasy and Possession: The Attraction of Women to the Cult of Dionysus," *The Harvard Theological Review,* v. 72, no. 1/2 (1979).

Kugelman, Richard, "The First Letter to the Corinthians," in Brown, Raymond E., Joseph A. Fitzmyer, and Roland E. Murphy (eds.) *The Jerome Biblical Commentary*. Prentice-Hall, Inc., 1968.

Kuhn, Thomas S. *The Copernican Revolution: Planetary Astronomy in the Development of Western Thought.* Harvard University Press, 1957.

Küng, Hans. (tr. Edward Quinn). *On Being a Christian.* Garden City, NY: Doubleday, 1976.

Kushner, Harold S. *When Bad Things Happen to Good People.* Random House, 1981.

Lanci, John R. "The Stones Don't Speak and the Texts Tell Lies: Sacred Sex at Corinth," in Schowalter, Daniel N. and Steven J. Friesen, eds. *Urban Religion in Roman Corinth.* Cambridge: Harvard Theological Studies #53, 2005, pp. 205-220.

Landon, Mark, " Beyond Peirene: Toward a Broader View of Corinthian Water Supply," in *Corinth, Vol. 20, Corinth, The Centenary: 1896-1996.* American School of Classical Studies at Athens (2003), pp. 43-62.

Lang, Mabel. *Cure and Cult in Ancient Corinth: A Guide to the Asklepieion.* Old Corinth Notes No. 1. Princeton, NJ: American School of Classical Studies at Athens, 1977.

Larson, Jennifer. *Greek Heroine Cults.* University of Wisconsin Press, 1995.

Lewis, M. J. T., "Railways in the Greek and Roman World," http://www.sciencenews.gr/docs/diolkos.pdf

Maccoby, Hyam. *The Mythmaker: Paul and the Invention of Christianity.* NY: Barnes & Noble, 1986.

MacDonald, Brian R. "The Diolkos," *The Journal of Hellenic Studies*, v. 106 (1986), pp. 191-195.

McDonald, William A. "Archaeology and St. Paul's Journeys in Greek Lands: Corinth," *The Biblical Archaeologist,* v. 5, no 3 (Sep. 1942), pp. 36-48.

Maier, Harry O. *The Social Setting of the Ministry as Reflected in the Writings of Hermas, Clement, and Ignatius.* Waterloo, Ontario: Wilfrid Laurier University Press, 1991.

Martin, Troy W. "Paul's Argument from Nature for the Veil in I Corinthians 11:13-15 . . ." *Journal of Biblical Literature,* v. 123, no. 1 (2004), pp. 75-84.

Mattusch, Carol C. "Corinthian Metalworking: The Forum Area," *Hesperia,* v. 46, no. 4 (1977), pp. 380-389.

Mazella, David. "Diogenes the Cynic in the Dialogues of the Dead of Thomas Brown, Lord Lyttelton, and William Blake," *Texas Studies in Literature and Language,* v. 48, no. 2, Summer 2006, pp. 102-122.

Merced-Ownbey, D. Jasmine, "Roman Isis and the Pendulum of Religious Tolerance in the Empire." http://inquiry.uark.edu/Merced_Final_for_Online11-08.pdf.

Metzger, Bruce M. "Considerations of Methodology in the Study of the Mystery Religions and Early Christianity," *The Harvard Theological Review,* v. 48, no. 1 (Jan. 1955), pp. 1-20.

Morgan, Chrales H., II. "Excavations at Corinth, 1936-37," *American Journal of Archaeology,* v. 41, no. 4 (1937), pp. 539-552.

Murray, Alexander S., *Manual of Mythology.* NY: Tudor Pub. Co., 1935.

Neils, Jenifer, "Others Within the Other: An Intimate Look at Hetairai and Maenads," in Cohen, Beth, ed. *Not the Classical Ideal: Athens and the Construction of the Other in Greek Art.* Leiden: Brill, 2000, pp. 203-226.

Newbold, R. F. "Fear of Sex in Nonnus' *Dionysiaca," Electronic Antiquity* Vol. 4 Issue 2 - April 1998, antiquity-editor@classics.Server.edu.au

Nygren, Anders (tr. Philip Watson). *Agape and Eros.* Rev. ed., Philadelphia: Westminster Press, 1953.

Olalla, Pedro. *Mythological Atlas of Greece*. Athens: Road Editions, 2002.

Orr, William F. and James Arthur Walther. *I Corinthians* (The Anchor Bible). Doubleday & Co., Inc., 1976.

Ovid. (tr. Henry T. Riley). *The Amours, Art of Love, Remedy of Love, and Minor Works.*. London: George Bell & Sons, 1893A.

Ovid, (tr. Henry T. Riley).*The Heroides, or Epistles of the Heroines, etc. of Ovid.* London: George Bell and Sons, 1893B.

Pagels, Elaine H. *The Gnostic Paul: Gnostic Exegesis of the Pauline Letters.* Fortress Press, 1975.

Pausanias, tr. W. H. S. Jones. *Description of Greece,* Volume I (Loeb Classical Library). New York: G. P. Putnam's, 1918.

Petropoulou, M. Z. *Animal Sacrifice in Ancient Greek Religion, Judaism, and Christianity.* Oxford, 2008.

Phillips, Marie. *Gods Behaving Badly* (a novel). Back Bay Books (Little, Brown), 2007.

Pinault, Jody Rubin. *Hippocratic Lives and Legends.* Leiden: E. J. Brill, 1992.

Pindar (tr. J. B. Bury). *The Isthmian Odes of Pindar.* London and New York: Macmillan, 1892.

Plutarch (tr. J. Dryden and A. H. Clough). *Plutarch's Lives.* (The Harvard Classics, Vol. 12). New York: P. F. Collier & Son, 1909.

Reesor, Margaret E., "Fate and Possibility in Early Stoic Philosophy," *Phoenix,* v. 19, no. 4 (1965), pp. 285-297.

Reesor, Margaret E., "Poion and Poiotes in Stoic Philosophy," *Phronesis,* v. 17, no. 3 (1972), pp. 279-285.

Renault, Mary. *The Last of the Wine* (a novel).Pantheon, 1956, Pocket Books, 1964.

Renault, Mary. *The Mask of Apollo* (a novel). New York: Pantheon Books, 1966.

Richardson, Rufus B. "A Group of Dionysiac Sculptures Found at Corinth," *American Journal of Archaeology,* v. 8, no. 3 (Jul-Sep, 1904), pp. 288-296.

Ridgeway, William, "Measures and Weights," in Whibley, Leonard (ed). *A Companion to Greek Studies.* Cambridge: University Press, 1905, pp. 438-444.

Rist, John M. "A Note on Eros and Agape in Pseudo-Dionysius," *Vigiliae Christianae,* v. 20, no. 4, 1966, pp. 235-243.

Robertson, A. and A. Plummer. *A Critical and Exegetical Commentary of the First Epistle of St. Paul to the Corinthians,* 2nd Ed. (ICC). Edinburgh: T. & T. Clark, 1914.

Robertson, Noel. "Orphic Mysteries and Dionysiac Ritual" in Cosmopoulos, Michael B., *Greek Mysteries: The Archeology and Ritual of Ancient Greek Secret Cults.* Routledge, 2003.

Robinson, Rachel Sargent. *Sources for the History of Greek Athletics in English Translation.* Chicago: Ares Publishers, 1981.

Rosner, Brian S. "Temple Prostitution in I Corinthians 6:12-20," *Novum Testamentum,* v. 40 Fasc. 4 (Oct. 1998), pp. 336-351.

Russell, Bertrand. *Wisdom of the West.* Crescent Books, Inc. (London: Rathbone Books, Ltd.), 1959.

Salmon, J. B. *Wealthy Corinth: A History of the City to 338 B.C.* Oxford: Clarendon Press, 1984.

Shaw, Bernard. *Androcles and the Lion.* Baltimore: Penguin Books, 1951.

Shepherd of Hermas (tr. Kirsopp Lake), in *The Apostolic Fathers,* Vol II. Cambridge, MA: Harvard University Press (Loeb Classical Library), 1913.

Smith, Dennis Edwin. "The Egyptian Cults at Corinth," *The Harvard Theological Review,*　　v. 70, no. 3/4 (Jul-Oct, 1977).

Smythe, Gonzalvo C. *Medical Heresies Historically Considered.* Philadelphia: Presley Blakiston, 1880.

Sourvinou-Inwood, Christiane. "Persephone and Aphrodite at Locri: A Model for Personality Definitions in Greek Religion," *The Journal of Hellenic Studies*, v. 98 (1978), pp. 101-121.

Stace, W. T. *A Critical History of Greek Philosophy.* London: Macmillan, 1920.

Stauffer, E., "agapáo, agápe, agapetós" in Bromiley, Geoffrey W. *Theological Dictionary of the New Testament, Abridged in One Volume* (Kittel and Friedrich). William B. Eerdmans Publishing Company/Paternoster Press, 1985, pp. 5-10.

Steiner, Ann, "Pottery and Cult in Corinth: Oil and Water at the Sacred Spring," *Hesperia,* v. 61, no. 3 (1992), pp. 385-408.

Stern, Henri, "Architecture, The History of Western: Early Christian," in *The New Encyclopaedia Britannica*, vol. 13, 1998, pp. 914-917.

Stevenson, James. *A New Eusebius.* S.P.C.K., 1957.

Strabo (tr. Horace L. Jones). *The Geography of Strabo.* (Loeb Classical Library) Cambridge: Harvard Univeristy Press, 1917-1933.

Sweet, Waldo E. *Sport and Recreation in Ancient Greece: A Sourcebook with Translations.* NY: Oxford U.P., 1987.

Temin, Peter. "The Economy of the Early Roman Empire," *Journal of Economic Perspectives*, v. 20, no. 1 (2006), pp. 133-151.
Tertullian, *Adversus Marcion.*

Theissen, Gerd. Tr. John W. Schutz. *The Social Setting of Pauline Christianity.* Philadelphia: Fortress Press, 1982.

Thiselton, Anthony C. *The First Epistle to the Corinthians: A Commentary on the Greek Text.* (The New International Greek Testament Commentary) Eerdmans, 2000.

Thompson, Cynthia L. "Hairstyles, Head-Coverings, and St. Paul: Portraits from Roman Corinth," *The Biblical Archaeologist,* v. 51, no. 2 (1988), pp. 99-115.

Thornton, Bruce S. *Eros: The Myth of Ancient Greek Sexuality.* Boulder, Co: Westview Press, 1997.

Toffler, Alvin. *Future Shock.* Random House, 1970.

Toynbee, Jocelyn M. C. "Architecture and Art in the Graceo-Roman World, 31 BC – AD 390," in Toynbee, Arnold, ed. *The Crucible of Christianity: Judaism, Hellenism and the Historical Background to the Christian Faith.* World Publishing Co., 1969, pp. 193-202.

Troupe, John Franklin. *St. Paul and the Mystery Religions.* Boston: The Gorham Press, 1917.

Turcan, Robert (tr. By Antonia Nevill). *The Cults of the Roman Empire.* Oxford: Blackwell, 1996.

Ure, A. D., "Demeter and Dionysos on Acrocorinth," *The Journal of Hellenic Studies,* v. 89 (1969).

Ven Kooten, George H. *Paul's Anthropology in Context* (Wissenschaftliche Untersuchungen zum Neuen Testament, 232), chapter 4, "Competition in the Christian communities in Corinth." Tübingen: Mohr Seibeck, 2008, pp. 246-249.

Virgil (tr. John Dryden). *Virgil's Aeneid.* (The Harvard Classics, Vol. 13). New York: P. F. Collier & Son, 1909.

Vitruvius. Tr. Morgan, M. H. *Vitruvius: The Ten Books on Architecture.* Cambridge: Harvard University Press, 1914.

Walbank, Mary E. Hoskins, "Aspects of Corinthian Coinage in the Late 1st and Early 2nd Centuries A.C. " in Williams, Charles K. II and Nancy Bookidis, eds. *Corinth: Results of Excavations, etc. Vol XX, Corinth: The Centenary, 1896-1996.* The American School of Classical Studies at Athens, 2003, pp. 337-349.

Wallraff, Barbara, "Word Court," *Atlantic Monthly,* June 2004, p. 154.

Weinberg, Saul S. and Gladys R. Weinberg. "Corinth: The Ancient City Revealed," *The Classical Journal.* vol. 42, no. 2, 1946, pp. 67-76.

Welborn, L. L. "On the Discord in Corinth: I Corinthians 1-4 and Ancient Politics," *Journal of Biblical Literature,* v. 106, no. 1 (1987), pp. 85-111.

West, Willis Mason. *The Ancient World from the Earliest Times to 800 A.D.* (Revised Edition). Boston: Allyn and Bacon, 1913.

Westermann, William Linn. *The Slave Systems of Greek and Roman Antiquity.* Philadelphia: The American Philosophical Society, 1955.

Williams, Charles K., II. "Roman Corinth: The Final Years of Pagan Cult Facilities along East Theatre Street," in Schowalter, Daniel N. and Steven J. Friesen, eds. *Urban Religion in Roman Corinth.* Cambridge: Harvard Theological Studies, #53, 2005, pp. 221-247.

Winter, Bruce W. *After Paul Left Corinth: The Influence of Secular Ethics and Social Change.* Wm. B. Eerdmans Publishing Co., 2001.

Witt, R. E. *Isis in the Ancient World* (also published as *Isis in the Graeco-Roman World* by Cornell U.P.). Johns Hopkins U.P., 1971.

Wyse, Thomas. *An Excursion in the Peloponnesus in the Year 1858,* vol. 2, London: Day & Son, 1865.

Yerkes, R. K. *Sacrifice in Greek and Roman Religion and in Early Judaism* (1952).

Zaidman, Louise Bruit and Pauline Schmitt Pantel (tr. Paul Cartledge). *Religion in the Ancient Greek City.* Cambridge University Press, 1992.

SCRIPTURE INDEX

GENERAL INDEX

About the Author

Richard Davies is a retired United Methodist minister with broad experience. In addition to 25 years as a pastor, he has worked as an ecumenical executive, and has taught in college and seminary. He and his wife, Elaine, are the proud parents of two adult children.

He earned his B.S. degree from New Mexico State University, and has degrees in theology from Garrett-Evangelical Theological Seminary, Evanston, Illinois, and Christian Theological Seminary, Indianapolis, Indiana. He received the Ph.D. degree from Indiana University, Bloomington, Indiana, where his special emphasis was "message design."

In 1984, he published a text-book, *Handbook for Doctor of Ministry Projects: An Approach to Structured Observation of Ministry*.

He and Elaine currently live in the Atlanta, Georgia metropolitan area.

Made in the USA
Charleston, SC
28 May 2010